THE
CENTURY
SPEAKS

# ULSTER
*voices*

A May Day parade in Belfast, 1960.

THE
CENTURY
SPEAKS

ULSTER
*voices*

*Memories of Ulster people*
*compiled by Owen McFadden from his interviews*
*for the* **BBC Northern Ireland** *series*
**The Century Speaks**

GILL & MACMILLAN

Published in Ireland by
Gill & Macmillan Ltd
Goldenbridge, Dublin 8
with associated companies throughout the world
Copyright © BBC Northern Ireland, 1999

ISBN 0 7171 3013 4

Typesetting and origination by
Tempus Publishing Limited
Printed in Great Britain by
Midway Clark Printing, Wiltshire

*For my mother and in memory of my father*

# CONTENTS

Paddy McAteer at the top of the Simplon Pass, Switzerland, 1954.

# ACKNOWLEDGEMENTS

I would like to thank all of the interviewees who shared their experiences with me throughout the making of *The Century Speaks*. Their stories never failed to fascinate, and the warmth with which they embraced the project was much appreciated.

I would also like to thank Arlene Huggins, who transcribed hours of interviews for this book, and Joanne Murphy, who helped knock the text into shape.

# INTRODUCTION

The story of life in Ulster this century has been dominated by political violence, a bloody conflict of identity and allegiance. Many of the interviewees featured in *The Century Speaks* vividly recalled the sectarian violence of the 1920s, the period which saw the birth of the state of Northern Ireland. The Troubles of the past thirty years obliterated much of the community spirit so fondly remembered by almost every speaker, and made Ulster a by-word for brutality and a seemingly insoluble dispute.

But throughout the century, life has gone on as elswhere. Heavy industry grew to dominate the capital city of this largely agricultural region. The Harland & Wolff shipyard employed up to 30,000 people at its peak, and Belfast was also able to boast of the world's largest linen industry and rope-works.

The welfare state transformed the lives of ordinary people – memories of the grinding poverty which scarred life in the twenties and thirties provide a stark reminder of today's relative affluence.

The technological revolution which continues apace has made life at home and in the workplace virtually unrecognizable from that at the beginning of the century, but the stoicism and humour of Ulster people remains unchanged. In their testimonies you will hear the warmth and comapssion which is the true voice of this place.

Owen McFadden
October 1999

George Heatherington and family in 1919. Ruby Purdy, aged five, is in the middle.

# CHAPTER 1

# Childhood and schooldays

Lina Graham with her mother, Everina
Crozier, in Ballinamallard, 1939.

William Hutton as a small boy in 1925.

## All Together

I was born in 20 Craigavad Street. I'm still in the same district, where I was born, and all the Somerville family were there – I was Somerville to my own name. They used to call it Somerville Row, because we were in 20, I'd an aunt in 14, I had an aunt in 28, my granda's house was 13 and I had an auntie in 7, and an uncle in 15 – all in the one street, so it was very good, like, you know, we were all together.

They all met in my granda's at night and he had a fender you know, across the open fire, and there was a board across it, and the young ones like us we used to fight who would get at each end of the fire, and it was always good crack, for there was no television or nothing then you see. And I had an uncle: he was good at telling yarns and things, and then they were all very good with their hands with knitting and embroidering and sewing and crochet, and it was just a gathering. The kids would have went in just to get a bit of a laugh, you know.

I had a brother and a sister who died when they were babies. I just faintly remember the boy, and I just had one brother; he was two years older than me, and we were very close. My father was a good father but he was in bad health, and didn't work, and in those days he didn't get any money or anything. My mother, she worked all her days, she brought the two of us up, you know. My father was willing enough to work, but he wasn't able.

*Nessie McNamee, born 1921*

## Baking

My grandmother was a great baker, you see: not cakes or buns or anything fancy, but potato bread, soda bread, oat cakes that kind of thing, so we got through. We were very respectable and we held on pretty well you know, and we managed pretty well.

*William Hutton, born 1921*

## Working Parents

I was born at No. 38 Ribble Street off the Newtownards Road, Belfast. That was a fairly respectable area because the houses were parlour houses, as they were called, and occupied principally by workers who were engaged in shipbuilding at Harland and Wolff and Workman Clarke shipbuilding firms.

My mother was born in Banbridge and she was a linen weaver. When she came to Belfast she worked in Ross's factory at East Bread Street, again off the Newtownards Road, and she was on high-class linen weaving at that time. Most of her work was done for Buckingham Palace, for King George V in those days.

My father, he was a foreman plater in Harland and Wolff's, he came from Barrow in Furness, in the North of England, Lancashire, and he came here and worked as a plater first of all. Then he was promoted finally to a foreman plater in charge of two squads, one in the main yard and one in the east yard. He had to travel between the yards, to keep the work going.

*Charles Murray, born 1908*

With Best Wishes 1935

William Hutton in 1935.

Charles Murray as a baby, with his mother, in 1908.

## Seeing the Yard as a Child

I was taken to the yard several times to see launches of ships. I can't remember the names of the ships but I can remember distinctly coming down and seeing them going down the slipway, and the crowds of men running to get onto the slipway too. They would lift the jelly in which the ship was launched – it was greased with a form of jelly – and this they used in their homes for black soap. It had certain qualities in it that were disinfectant so they used it in their homes.

Always a company director or a member of the royal family came along to launch the ship. There might have been about 30,000 men employed in Harland and Wolff's at that time, and the remarkable thing about it was that they would never launch a ship on Friday the 13th of the month – it was always postponed to the following Monday, but was never launched on Friday the 13th. They had a feeling about it.

*Charles Murray, born 1908*

## Early Memories

I didn't always live in Lewis Street. My mother lived over where the Lodge Road is; then it was all Protestants, in 1919. Then in '21 we had to move; the people who were in our house in Lewis Street were Catholic, so they had to get out, and we were Protestants so we had to come in, so that's how we were there. There was my grandmother and my uncle who wasn't married and my mother, father and the five of us – my sister and I and three brothers – we all lived there. There was a big attic in the house so there was plenty of room. My father was a cabinetmaker, and I remember he got his fingers all off with the circular saw, he got the tips of his fingers off.

It was a hard time but, at the same time, we didn't lose anything I think, you know we were content. I remember my mother would have bought us something maybe on a Friday. Maybe it was alphabet sweets and she'd bought a quarter and we would have all sat round the table and tried to make names. As I say, my father being a cabinet maker, there was always little bits of blocks about, so my brothers they would have built things. I remember my grandmother always baked, she baked on the fire, on the griddle so we always had fresh bread and she'd say, 'now I'm boiling this cabbage and its good for you and you eat it', or 'I'm boiling this turnip and you'll eat it because its good for you', so you had to take it, and you didn't dare say no. We were always together, so I think that made a difference too. I mean, the children now, they're going out and they get money for to go here and there; we were at home and we were happy to be there.

*Isobel Cobain, born 1919*

## Lagan Locks

I was born at Stranmillis. In those days there was just a village at the very end of what we called the tramlines and there were just three streets of houses. The rest was all fields and allotments and all that kind of thing, and there was

Margaret Mills as a young girl in Stranmillis, Belfast, in 1925.

the river Lagan just beside us. And we as children would have went down onto the riverbank; the river was tidal then – it's not tidal now – and when the tide went out we used to go down to the river, and paddle about in it. Some of the boys would have swam in the river, and then the first locks were there. The barges came up from the coal quay and the sand quay and there was grain barges and they came up, a tug brought them, and we called it the *Maggie*, whether that was the name or not. But this tug brought the barges up to the first lock and then the men had big long poles and they pushed the barges into the lock. They went through the lock then, and we children used to love to go down to the locks when the barges where going through, and the men were very nice to us, very tolerant of us, and you know in a lock there's a big long thing for pushing it open and closed and we used to think we were helping you know, whenever we put our backs to it. But anyway then when it was through the lock there was a canal. That Lagan canal now is no longer there; it's filled in. A horse then would have linked up to the barge and would have taken it on up to the next lock, which was at Shaw's bridge.

Those three streets were mostly for workers: they were people that were employed in the Vulcanite and the brickyard, there was a brickfield there. Vulcanite Ltd was a felt works and they were very busy during the First World War because they made felt for the trenches. I remember watching the men putting the bricks in and out of the kilns, the things to harden the bricks.

The streets were Wansbeck Street, Laganvale Street and Harleston Street, and they called it the Laganvale village; we were termed as a village in those days because there was nothing else round us. There was the soup factory there as well – Edwards' soup factory – and all the men in those three streets worked in one of those places.

*Margaret Mills, born 1918*

## Childhood Illness

I had a lot of illnesses when I was young, and at school. When I was nine I took a severe illness, I took a lump in my neck here which was quite common in those days. I remember I was off school from Hallowe'en to the following Easter with this thing in my neck. My mother took me to Professor H.P. Hall who was down about University Street and when he looked at it, he said, 'I won't take it out here' – he was going to lance it – 'I won't take it out here, I'll do it in your own home.' He came the next day with these big drums of dressings, and put a white apron and all on. It frightened me really, but he took this lump out of my neck in the house; I mean they don't do that kind of thing now. My father hadn't a very big pay and it would have been five guineas but the Professor said he would do it for three, so you got it for three guineas, and of course we had doctors' bills and all to pay in those days. The doctor came from the Mater hospital, that's where he lived, and he took a tram from the Mater hospital to Stranmillis to dress my wound every day. So really doctors didn't all have cars and things in those days.

*Maud Meneely, born 1929*

16

Margaret Mills (right) with her parents and sister in Belfast.

The Meneely family at the old farm building in Tempo, Co. Fermanagh.

## On the Farm

I grew up on a farm just outside Tempo. My father was a small farmer and I was the seventh daughter of a family of nine, and I just had one brother younger than myself. It was quite a gathering, but the funniest thing is looking back I never remember us all being in the same room at the same time, because there was quite an age difference obviously between us, and by the time I was a child my older sisters where away working, away from home. No matter what event happened in the family – a death or a marriage – there seemed to be always somebody missing.

I was the seventh child and the seventh daughter on a farm, so I don't think they were too pleased to see me. They wanted a boy obviously for to carry on the farm, and then he came next, he was the eighth and then I had another sister, the ninth.

*Maud Meneely, born 1929*

## Street Games

We used to be fond of playing the film stars in those days, and we'd let on I was Janette McDonald and another was Bibi Daniels. We used to have good fun playing that. I loved playing ball and two balls and that, and we used to get chased for playing up against the side wall of a house. And then there were a lot of wee shops in the street that were in the houses, you know, just wee shops. They would have had the window and we used to play 'I spy with my little eye' – we would have went all round the wee shop window. I think it was a very happy childhood; like I might have had it hard, but it was happy. I think we were happier then than they are now, the kids.

*Nessie McNamee, born 1921*

## Mother and Father

They were just quiet ordinary farmers: very, very hard working, because in those days there was very little machinery of any kind, everything was done more or less by hand, no tractors or anything like that. We had a couple of horses and it was very hard work, and hard for my mother as well. She didn't only work out on the farm but as well as that, you know, she cooked just on the hearth fire in the beginning, before we got a range, and in the summer that must have been tremendous. You know how hot it was working over a fire, to feed a big family. It was a very small farm, it wouldn't have been more than forty acres and mixed farming – most small farmers

were like that then. We had everything from cows to pigs to hens to turkeys – whatever.

*Maud Meneely, born 1929*

## Family

My father was a very loveable man. He was very quiet and he was heavy built and his mother had sixteen children. Eleven of them lived, the rest were miscarriages and that kind of thing. My mother was more of a socialite, she liked to socialize and have friends in and she brought us up very well, and made us speak well, and made us have good manners and all that kind of thing, she was strict, she was very strict. But my father wasn't: he was more of a loveable kind of man. However, they got on very well together the two of them. I would say I suppose she ruled the roost.

*Margaret Mills, born 1918*

## Moving to Belfast

I was born in West Cumbria but my mother was from Belfast, and I was just over nine years of age when I first came over here with my mother, because my father had died at that time, and I settled down into Belfast. So in reality I'm a Belfast man or an Ulster man or an Irish man, in that I've lived here for so long. I go back to my old home town as often as I can. Of course, it's on the fringe of the Lake District and, being a walker as well as a cyclist, the English Lake District is a

Maud Meneely's mother, father and sister, Olive, in Tempo, Co. Fermanagh.

Paddy McAteer and friends outside Buttermere Youth Hostel in the Lake District, July 1962. From left to right: Ken Blair, John Corry, Paddy McAteer, David Oldham, John Reilly, Elliot Matthews.

tremendous attraction. It's like Mecca for walkers, in a sense that if you live in these islands some time or other you'll go to the Lake District.

It was a big setback to me, because I was coming back to a different culture if you like, and particularly so in those days, that would be 1937. My goodness, there's such a difference between then and now. Basically when I came over here what really struck me, amazed me really, was the tribality of it all, you know the various tribes, and I took a long time to come to terms with that. I felt that I was different, and I felt that I wanted to stay as a different person, on the basis that I didn't want to be one or the other. And even at that early age I had that feeling there was something wrong in society here. People were very friendly and, you know, enjoyable, but that terrible gap, that terrible distance between the cultures was something I found very hard to come to terms with. I of course had been brought up in an English atmosphere in a school that had all creeds and types and whatever, and of course over there religion is not a factor, or wasn't, and suddenly I came here and I had to go to the local school.

*Paddy McAteer, born 1928*

## 'The Holy Land'

It was called the 'Holy Land' because you had Carmel Street, Palestine Street, Jerusalem Street, Damascus Street, Penrose Street all the places in the Holy Land, then I think for a time there that people didn't refer to it as such, they'd all sorts of other names for it, but it has reverted back to that now.

I would say each street, I suppose, had its own sort of little situations and people, personalities and what have you, but as a whole I think it would have been quite a good community. We knew all the neighbours; granted, your house was much closer together than a semi-detached or detached villa would be, and you certainly had no back garden to sit in, so you came out to your front door, where people would be passing and you'd talk to them. You were involved with people's lives, help or what have you. I suppose we had our scandals, we had our problems, but for instance if there was a death, there was a collection, somebody went round and collected to provide a wreath and you were invited to go in and view the body, and in some cases people would have gone in and even had a drink and that with them. But to me it was certainly closer, you were in closer touch with people and as I say you helped where you could, if anybody came for help and that. Even though we were much in the same state as far as the financial end of it was concerned. We had taxi drivers and people that worked in the bakery and the few industrial places that there were round about, they would have worked in them.

*Peg Armstrong, born 1919*

## Corner Shops

My mother would have been strict, my father would have indulged me and spoiled me, and would have taken my part, not against my mother really. Then of course I had a grandmother across the road, and my grandmother lived in No. 42 with two maiden aunts then. One of them did eventually get married. So grandmother she again was the spoiler: she came over and I always remember about one time I would have been about four years old, and grandmother came to take me round the corner for sweets. Then, again, we had all the little shops – almost every corner had a shop at it selling confectionery and also groceries and that, so you met there in the little shops. And my grandmother came and my mother had told me that my lunch was nearly ready. She said come round for sweets, so of course off I went with my grandmother. When I got back again my mother said to me that she had told me that the lunch was ready and I had gone off with my grandmother. She got my father's strop for his razor which he hung behind the door, she got that and she gave me a few taps on the legs. My mother would have been a great one for remembering your manners and not doing anything that would disgrace the family.

*Peg Armstrong, born 1919*

## Track Laying

One of the interesting things I think that happened in those days was the laying down of the first tramway track on the Newtownards Road. I can remember half the school being off with flash trouble in their eyes, due to watching the welders welding together the rails in the road. Our school wasn't a large school; it didn't have much room for physical activity, we had no sports whatever but the only exercise we ever got was inside the classroom itself between lessons, but that wasn't uncommon in those days. Schools were sprouting up all over the place and this was a very common factor.

I remember the Holywood Arches very well and, if I might say so, I remember one shop called the Victory that was just below the Arches. The name of the people was Cunningham, who owned the Victory shop, it was a big confectioner shop.

*Charles Murray, born 1908*

## Uncle's Crystal Set

This thing as I remember was in a kind of a box and he kept it in the corner. He worked more often to try and get the two little levers – there was like a piece of crystal actually sitting in the middle – and you had to work these little levers to actually get something. Of course you got awful sounds and that, you've earphones, but I mean I don't remember a lot of programmes, my memory is of brass bands, and he was very keen on that, so that suited him beautifully. I suppose there was news and things like that on it, but I just don't remember exactly.

*Peg Armstrong, born 1919*

## Hostelling

Towards the end of the forties a few friends and I, we knocked about and had nothing much to do. We did a bit of cycling, we were always involved in the cycling world, and we discovered someone told us about youth hostelling and we decided to give it a try, because we'd got basically fed up with just running about, like almost corner boys, and we wanted to get out into the countryside again. I know I did because it was in my blood, coming from Portstewart.

We decided that we would try youth hostelling and the first hostel we went to was a place called Whitestown in County Louth very near to Carlingford. It was a very, very simple old farmhouse and we cooked with a primus stove, which was basically a paraffin oil stove. We had oil lamps for lighting, there wasn't any heating. There was a big fire in the place but when you went to bed what you had was a sort of a straw palliasse. But there was a camaraderie about the place, and it was enjoyable, and for quite a number of years afterwards I hostelled every weekend, and that included the winter season at Christmas.

*Victor Douglas, born 1931*

## Harland and Wolff

It was the middle of the war, August 1942. So the war was well and truly on, the Blitz was over, and they had rebuilt some of the factories that had been damaged during the air raids and they were in full production. I don't

Girls rehearsing for a Command Performance attended by the Princess Royal (later Queen Elizabeth) in 1945. Sheila Hughes is in the centre.

think they ever were busier than they were during the Second World War, because of the depletion or the constant loss of merchant and naval ships to the U-boats and the elements of course which were always present. So the shipyard was very, very busy.

To a small boy it was not so much daunting as exciting. The small group that was starting on that particular day as indentured apprentices were ultimately taken by a messenger boy through various workshops with instructions to leave this one here and that one there, and passing through those workshops it was really quite something to see huge diesel engines. You had to go through the iron foundry and see the huge buckets of molten metal and so on, and the very, very lofty buildings and overhead cranes and quite a lot of noise, it was really quite something, it was very, very exciting, and perhaps a little daunting.

*William Austin, born 1926*

## Childhood in the Theatre

I didn't realise that my life in a way was different to anybody else's but I suppose it was quite different, in that you know, I was absorbed into the family atmosphere of theatre if I can get that across to you, right from a very young age. I can remember back as far the age of two when an old music hall artist came called Florrie Ford who was playing the Empire at the time, she gave me a present of a toy penguin which I still have, and I can remember very well her giving me that you know, at that time.

*Sheila Hughes, born 1928*

## St Barnabas' School

I went to St Barnabas' School which was in the Duncairn Gardens. My sister and I and we had no problems going to school, we liked it. We always had to go to Sunday school and I remember my granny, she used to get dressed on Sunday with her 'dog skin jacket', as she called it, and her hat, and walk up to St Barnabas'. So we went there but you didn't rebel about going to Sunday school or anything you know, you went there and you went to school too. You took your penny and it was a big open fire, and I liked it. I remember getting my writing displayed in a glass case and she bought me a silver medal out of Sharman D. Neill's in the town, and there was a gold heart in it.

I loved school, loved school no problem at all. You were made to do your... they said exercise; I guess its homework now. It was your exercise when you came in and you had to do it before you travelled any further.

*Isobel Cobain, born 1919*

## Walking to School

I went to what was then called a public elementary school, and it was a school called Coolkelly out in the country. I think the walk must have been five to six miles to school over fields, roads, a river, a bog, you name it. We walked to school, summer and winter, through that. It's wonderful looking back, but it wasn't so nice at the time, really, you know: but we still enjoyed it walking to school, because there was always something to see. We watched out for the birds in the summertime and the springtime. We used to go into somebody's orchard and have a couple of apples on the way and different things like that – it was a bit of an adventure, I suppose, looking back.

I loved school, but my brother hated school, and it was a problem getting him there. My sister and myself had to hold him by the hand all the way; if we let go he ran back home again. He hated school and he wouldn't do his homework. And our teacher, when he didn't do his homework, she blamed me as well. I was supposed to make him do it, so he got slapped and I got slapped as well, so that wasn't so nice. But I enjoyed the work at school, I loved school, and I would have loved to have been able to go on to university or something like that, but for us at the time that just wasn't an option, because it cost money in those days, you know, to do that kind of thing.

*Maud Meneely, born 1929*

## Christian Brothers' School

Because my mother was Catholic I had to go to a Christian Brothers' school, and I might say it was a good school, and the teachers were wonderful, and I got a grand education. But I felt that I was being caged in: I just couldn't accept the reality of the situation, that I was Catholic and I had to go to a Catholic school, and everybody around me was Catholic and everyone had the same outlook on things relative to the situation at that time.

We were settled right in the centre, in the city end of North Queen Street,

and that was good for me in many ways. I wasn't in a ghetto at that time, and I was able to walk out the front door and I was right into Donegal Street and in the city centre, and that was a solace – that was a good thing for me.

*Paddy McAteer, born 1928*

## McClure Street

My first school was down at McClure Street where my mother had gone to school. She came from around Donegall Pass and she had gone to McClure Street School, and of course thought that I ought to go there too. I was there for a while and then I was always complaining to my grandmother and she was always coming round to say, 'I don't see why you can't send the child round the corner to Rea Memorial', which is in Rugby Avenue.

*Peg Armstrong, born 1919*

## School Clothes

I spent my schooldays in a little hut, you'd call it a hut now. It was just a little building with only one room, there was the teacher in one end, there was a teacher in the other end. I went to school when I was four and a half, according to what my mother told me. But in those days the girls wore pinafores, all lovely white embroidered pinafores, and the girl who sat beside me, she was an only child and I used to very envious, She used to come with the most beautiful clothes, where I was coming with the hand-me-downs, but I

Maud Meneely's mother, Mary Forde.

Four scenes of Margaret Mills and friends celebrating her twenty-first birthday.

Class III of Belmont Public Elementary School in 1925. Ruby Purdy is sixth from the left on the third row.

didn't mind. So this particular day I was feeling bad about things, and when I came home I said to mother, 'You know, Bertha had a new dress on today again.' 'Oh dear, oh dear,' she says, but she says 'Your life and Bertha's life is two different things: she has nobody to play with', and that put a different aspect on it for me. After that I didn't pay any attention to her clothes – I paid my attention to the girl.

*Lena Purdy, born 1901*

# CHAPTER 2
# *Work*

William Hutton aged eighteen.

William Hutton (left) working in the Harland & Wolff insurance office, 1953.

## Harland and Wolff

When I joined Harland and Wolff's there were 30,000 workers there. There were more men in one yard – Musgrave Yard – than the whole of John Brown's in Glasgow, and it was a fairly big concern, 30,000 workers. It was a world all of its own and it really was seven days a week. Well, workers could have taken a Sunday off, but we had to be there as timekeepers, to be there to keep the time and do the wages.

There was a man called Billy Towell.

Now Billy started as an apprentice plumber in the late twenties, and like I said there was very little shipbuilding going on, so what they did, they put the apprentices to cleaning windows. So these boys were all cleaning the windows and one of them said, 'look, I broke one of those windows there', he said. I broke the glass out of it and looking from the ground you wouldn't know there wasn't any glass in the window. So somebody said come on we'll break the whole lot of them, so they went along and broke every window in the row, and the foreman came round and he looked and he said, 'you've made a good job of these windows, you wouldn't see a mark on them.' Well, later on then shipbuilding did pick up and Billy was put to work with a plumber, an older man. Billy said, 'We were carrying a big pipe on our shoulders along the deck and the lights went out. So the plumber said over his shoulder, "look, we've only to go round the next bulkhead, the next corner, and there's no use leaving this pipe down. I'll light a match, and you follow on." So he lit a match, but he came to an open manhole in the deck. He didn't say to me, "look out, there's an open manhole", he walked round it and I walked down it. Well,' Billy said, 'they say your life passes before you when you're falling like that, and its true my whole life up to then passed before me, and I landed in the bottom, and I lay there in the dark, and then the next thing I heard men coming down with lamps looking for me. They went into the wrong hold, and I shouted "I'm not in there, I'm in here." So they came down and they gathered round me, in the light of these lamps and one of them said, "Good gracious, son, can you get on my back?" Another man said, "He's not going to get on your back, we don't know what injuries he has." Then the lights came on and they lowered down a stretcher and they got me onto the

A group of Harland & Wolff's Timekeeping and Wages staff, Alexandra Works section, c. 1953. William Hutton is on the extreme left.

33

stretcher, but my arms were free. They lifted me up in a crane, you see, and I was spinning round, and there was a scaffolding where men had been working at staging; and I put out my arm to save myself off the staging and a pain shot up my arm. It was only then that I knew I had a broken arm. I got off with a broken arm and two staved ankles.'

But then Billy had a great religious experience you see – conversion. He looked at the shipyard and he said, '30,000 workers, what a mission field, I have to do something about this.' Now there were pockets of Bible classes here and there about the shipyard, but Billy went to work and he went round all the yards, and he got them all organized into committees, each one a unit on its own looking after. They had these open-air religious services in the lunch hour, and Sir Frederick Rebbick, the top man in the shipyard, came down one day and he listened to these. After he listened to them he gave the order that all their equipment – microphones and what have you – were to be serviced in the company's time and at the company's expense.

*William Hutton, born 1921*

## The Shipyard

What happened was that I had a brother who went to work as an apprentice fitter in Craig's of Great Georges Street, which is still there, there's still a wee engineering firm there now. And they did a whole lot of millwright work, and that was working mills, like the Gallaher's tobacco factory and the linen mills and that, they would do big engineering installation of machinery and that. I remember then it was a five-year that you had to do to serve your time. You had to sign indentures and you had five years to do. When he finished his time my brother went to sea as an engineer with a company, Alfred Holt and Company, which was the famous 'blue funnel line'. I then of course was influenced by that, because what happened was he would then have other seamen and engineers coming up to visit him when he was home on leave, and you would then be listening to that talk and listening about them doing this and doing that, and the places that they'd been. And I think that that started to influence me quite a bit. The other thing about it, of course, was due to my relatively poor performance at school, I had a limited choice of what I had to do. And I think that that's an important thing, you were that limited, the less qualifications you had, the more limited the choices of what you can do. He was at sea for quite a considerable period of time, and he then ultimately went into the shipyard as a manager and that, but that was after I'd started in there. But of course then I had an influence, and this is the point that I was making earlier on. This was the father, son or brother influence as to what you did as a career, or what you moved into.

*Clive Hughes, born 1939*

## First Day at the Shipyard

You had at that time to go down and get an examination and then if you

THE GOVAN SHIPBUILDING YARD, GLASGOW.

DIESEL ENGINE WORKS, FINNIESTON, GLASGOW.

DIESEL ENGINE WORKS, SCOTSTOUN, GLASGOW.

CLYDE FOUNDRY, GOVAN, GLASGOW.

SHIPBUILDING YARD, GREENOCK.

SHIP REPAIRING & ENGINEERING WORKS,
LONDON, LIVERPOOL
AND
SOUTHAMPTON.

IA COCKSPUR STREET,
LONDON, S.W.I.

HARLAND AND WOLFF, LIMITED.

TELEGRAMS: HARLANDIC, BELFAST.

TELEPHONE: 3339.

*Shipbuilding & Engineering Works,*

*Belfast,* 13th December, 1930.

ALL COMMUNICATIONS TO BE ADDRESSED TO THE COMPANY.

TO WHOM IT MAY CONCERN.

 This is to certify that Mr. C. Murray entered our employment as an apprentice turner on the 29th May, 1924, and was transferred to the Engine Works Drawing Office on 1st August, 1928, where he completed his apprenticeship on the 22nd June, 1929.

 He remained in our employment until the present date, being principally engaged on pipe arrangements and details for same.

 We have found him painstaking and reliable, and, having regard to his years and experience, a good draughtsman. His conduct and time-keeping have been satisfactory.

 Owing to the depressed state of the industry we regret we have to dispense with his services.

     For HARLAND AND WOLFF, LIMITED.

      *F. Eneblech*

      MANAGING DIRECTOR.

HB.
30.

An all too common letter from the early years of the Great Depression.

passed the examination you were taken on as an apprentice. And I remember my mother getting me organized, to start with to go down the yard. And that time there, hobnailed boots really were in style, big heavy boots, you know. They weren't the industrial boots that you have now, with steel toe caps on them, but they were heavy boots and my mother got me these pair of heavy boots. And she got me two ex-army shirts from Millets which was in High Street then I think, and boiler suits which were still too big – she thought I was going to grow into them, even though by that time I was six foot two. So I spent my first year with rolled up-boiler suits (but that was beside the point!) and a lunchbox. And I can remember very well starting the first day, and there wasn't an introduction, you went down the same way and you signed your indentures. Some of the apprentices went into stores for very short periods of time to acclimatize them, but in actual fact I went right on to the shop floor then. And it was not an easy time, because to start with, and I know it seems silly, you had to stand for eight hours, and I mean at school you didn't have to stand, you just had to sit for eight hours, maybe, but certainly not stand for eight hours. And I found that, as a young boy growing up, quite difficult. The man that I was sent to work with, and it was nearly on a one to one you worked as an apprentice, wasn't a particularly nice person, and of course I started to have grave doubts about just what kind of career I'd chosen, and was it maybe what I wanted to do. That was accumulated, it was an accumulation of factors as well, because the sun was beating down in August and the

workshop I was in was red hot. I had my mother's ex-army shirt on, plus a boiler suit and it was hot and uncomfortable. And the first few days I would have had that kind of feeling of not being very happy.

*Clive Hughes, born 1939*

## Trouble Finding Work

It was a bad time to look for work because many places were without work so it was pretty hopeless. I tried everywhere, and I even, should I say, walked from the labour exchange right to Ballygowan trying to hire myself out as a farmhand at labouring on a farm and couldn't do it. It was a stressful time because at my home, my father was out, I was out myself, my brother was out and my sister was the only one working and she was working in the Albion clothing company, earning about 8s 6d a week.

Another time I left the exchange and I went to Tombe Street to a vacancy that was there in Munster and Simms. Their head office was in Tombe Street at the time, and I was told that for the work in which I was trained they had no vacancies and that knocked me out. I couldn't go home; I took it so much to heart that I walked and walked and I don't remember walking one step of the way until I came to myself sitting down on the side of the road, between Newtownards and Dundonald, up in the Holywood Hills, and that's when I came to myself and I found that I was closer to Newtownards than I was to Belfast. So I walked in to Newtownards to friends of our own who saw me and got

36

Lina Graham with her mother, Everina Crozier, in Ballinamallard.

my hands and face washed and got food into me and put me on McCartney's bus in the square in Newtownards and sent me home again.

*Charles Murray, born 1908*

## Public Assistance

There was such a thing as Public Assistance and when we applied for it an officer came out and he saw the piano in the house and he said, 'That's a luxury, that'll have to go, sell that', and he saw the His Master's Voice gramophone, which my father had presented to him, and he said, 'That's also a luxury, sell that.' So gradually our house was being reduced in its furnishings just to keep things going.

I was out for two and a half years, my father was out longer, three years, so I got work before he did. I got a letter from Munster and Simms from a Mr Eaves and he asked me to come for an interview. I went for an interview and he told me what ideas he had in respect of a new lamp.

*Charles Murray, born 1908*

## Careers Advice

Careers advice in schools and that was greatly restricted, there wasn't a careers service. In a lot of cases you followed what a brother did, or a father did. You know you went into those occupations, maybe now and again others would drift into other occupations. But that was mainly what it was, some of the families were better

off, were maybe getting young people to university and sending them there. But there wasn't the same university attendance or anything like that.

*Clive Hughes, born 1939*

## Gallahers

I remember going and Mr Yeats, you had to hold out your hand and they touched your hand to see if it was moist or damp because you couldn't hold the cigarettes then. I went in and it was hand-packing then. You lifted them and you had to be gentle with them and put them in tins, then later on I went up and I was in the stripping room. The leaf came in from South Africa or Virginia and you had to strip the leaves off the stem and it went into like a nosebag beside you, it wasn't a very nice job, but the girls were nice. In Gallahers you had music while you worked and they had the ten o'clock: the milk came round, you got a little bottle of milk. So I was happy in my work.

It was a big factory and certainly they looked after their workers and we got lots of benefits. There was one machine, you had to feed the machine to make the cigarettes. Well, the bottom end of it had to be lifted up and the tobacco had to be thrown into this, and it was pitched into this and closed and then you fed it on paper, and it came through and then it chopped off. Then somebody was up at the other end grabbing these cigarettes and putting them on a stand, picking them out if there were loose ends or anything and throwing that out. But it wasn't really noisy because you'd heard the music, in

Lina Graham in Ballinamallard, 1950s.

Lina Graham with friend Anna and an RUC officer in Ballinamallard.

the hand-packing it wasn't noisy at all.

I think they did Senior Service and they did Amber Tip – these were beautiful expensive ones, I used to buy them for my husband at Christmas time then. They were like a wax end, they were nice. To go foreign it was Three Birds, this was during the wartime, and they were put into little round cans that would hold fifty. They'd say, 'Hurry up now, 'cause the boat's there down in the yard waiting on this order to get away.'

*Isobel Cobain, born 1919*


## Small Wages

I remember the uncle that lived with us he was going to get a job in Gallahers and he asked them how many times a week they paid him, the wages were so bad.

*Isobel Cobain, born 1919*


## Gertie's Typing Pool

I went back to the dreaded Gertie's typing pool but by this time I had started out as a Grade 2 typist, I got up to Grade 1, and then I was Grade 2 shorthand typist and Grade 1 shorthand typist, and I was on a different footing at that time. I used to go out to all the different offices and take shorthand, and then come back and type mostly letters and reports of meetings. I managed to get away again and I was then sent to Springfield Road and I worked for the detectives there.

*Lina Graham, born 1931*


## Working for the RUC

It was great fun and they were so good and they were very protective of me because I had just come up from the country and they kept an eye on me. I can remember one in particular: Paddy O'Hagan, he had relatives who sent him cake and Paddy and I used to have tea parties. When he got a cake he would invite me for tea. The trouble with Paddy was, he would pour the tea into his hand put it into a pot, fill it with cold water and stew it on the stove, and you never tasted tea like it. The cake was good. He was kind to me, they were all very kind to me, they were all great, I enjoyed working for them.

There was this character called Ronnie and Ronnie was one of those people who could walk out onto the street and see a man coming up the street carrying a radio, or whatever it was, and he knew immediately it was stolen, and he would bring him in.

There was a lot of things that they shielded me from – a lot of naughty goings-on shall we say, a lot of them statements, I never seen them – they did them themselves, because they felt I shouldn't know about things.

I remember we had a character called Alec who worked in the pawnshop across the road, he was hilarious. If you ever wanted anything you went over and Alec got it for you.

I'd got this idea actually when I worked in Enniskillen I wanted to join, but my boss told me, he said, 'You join,' he says, 'I'll take you round to the tide there and push you in.' I had wanted to join but I never really got around to it. I think perhaps the hours and I'd seen some of the things that they had to do.

There were very few policewomen then and things weren't as good as they are now for them. I wouldn't say they're equal now but they're a bit more equal, if you know what I mean. But in those days they were very much in the background, and they didn't do too much. They didn't do the more exciting things.

I thought I would like to wear the uniform and I thought I would like to get on. I thought that it was interesting to find out the things that happened and to do something about it, you know they did a lot of good work in those days. There were children that were being abused and they were taken away from those homes and their parents who abused them were prosecuted for it. It seemed to be children who were abused; I thought I would like to do something about that, I just had a feeling about it.

*Lina Graham, born 1931*

## Police in the Community

At that time you had the people in Clonard and there was great co-operation between them and the police, and even later than that, when my friend was kidnapped from a station. When she was leaving to go home one evening she was kidnapped and taken to a house in the Springfield Road area. Of course when she was found to be missing the police contacted the brothers and the nuns and they scoured the area. The fact that they did actually call at the house where she was scared them off, and they ran off and left her there, they got frightened. So there was always a great deal of co-operation

between the police and all the churches in the area.

*Lina Graham, born 1931*

## Being Transferred

I was transferred to headquarters in Waring Street which I didn't like, and said so being me, I was then transferred to York Road. I did a lot of court of enquiries then and if you knew shorthand they use they to do all that sort of thing. From there I went to Willowfield, and then to headquarters, and then moved from Willowfield to Castlereagh, so I was there for quite a long time. The work did change because when I got to Castlereagh I became a personal assistant and I had to make appointments and if you're working for a senior officer you do a lot of appointments and you talk to a lot of people and you make sure he doesn't talk to some of them.

*Lina Graham, born 1931*

## The RUC and the Troubles

At that time things were hotting up and there was a tricolour in a window and there was a lot of nastiness about that, it really was awful. It was very frightening actually because the crowds were out and they were breaking windows, and we were picking up the pieces.

To my mind it was really the very beginning of the Troubles in the city and it just escalated from there on. Mr Paisley was involved in that: he was up there directing operations, and protesting about the presence of the tricolour.

It was very scary because you never knew who was who and whether you were reliable. It didn't really matter: it was coming at you from both sides. You as the police were piggy in the middle again, and we were advised not to give anyone our telephone number, we were advised to close the blinds, to never sit in a room with the light on and the blinds not closed. I'm afraid I still find myself getting up and closing the blinds, and there were times when I got the odd funny telephone call and I would wonder whether it was just a coincidence or whether it was somebody who was actually targeting me, because of my connections. There were times when going in and out was a bit frightening too, because you never knew who was there, and there were times when if there was something on you would have the mob around and you really didn't want to be seen going in.

*Lina Graham, born 1931*

## Followed Home

I was giving a friend a lift home from the speakers' circle and I realized that I had been followed by a white car, and I had noticed the car the previous Monday night, I had noticed a white car behind. It didn't register until the second Monday night that at the same time as I came out a white car followed me. I turned into the estate and lost them, I actually stopped and went in to my friend's house for while and we looked outside to see and there was

nothing, and the place seemed to be clear. It had followed me and then driven on, and then I got back out and got home again. It probably was nothing but the fact that you were working in those circumstances, it was really really frightening, cause you probably blew things up out of all proportion.

*Lina Graham, born 1931*

## Friends and the Police

It was really rather dreadful, so it was. I can remember a young lad I had met in the depot and he was sitting in a remote country station and they came up and shot him through the letter box, as he sat at a desk. That is one thing I will always remember. Then another friend of mine from Ballinamallard who grew up opposite me, he was in Glengormley and he was trying to prevent a robbery and they shot him too. It was really dreadful when your friends were shot and it made you very angry to think that they would single them out and shoot them. That's only two – there were dozens of them, people that I knew.

There was a lot of anger around, but there was also a great spirit of camaraderie and people were together. I felt 'Well, I'm not alone', everybody else is facing this as well, so it was a time of great friendship really, because everybody had to depend on everybody else. I mean if you didn't have friends you were lost.

*Lina Graham, born 1931*

## Working at the Mill

It was a bit of a novelty, running about in your bare feet, and then you had to have what you called an apron tied round you, to catch the water. You thought you were great being a doffer, but there was no such thing as tea breaks or anything like that. What happened there was, there was no flasks or nothing like that years ago. People brought a can of tea with them, and if you got an interlude between that, you got a wee taste, if not you didn't. Now the foreman you daren't have let him see that, you'd have got the sack for that, so you got the wee cups of tea in between. Through it all we were all happy for we were doing that, it was on the sly, and if you got a biscuit it was a miracle, it was always pieces of jam and pieces of this.

And everybody was kindly, everybody shared, we got our two nights a week out. They would have said, 'Are you going out tonight? Will you lend us your coat?', if you had a decent coat. Well, that girl would have lent you her good coat, somebody else would have lent you something, so you would be good-looking going out that night, and you gave that back the next day, that's the way life went on. Many a time I wore another girl's coat for to go out dressed up.

When I went in first I went in as a wee cager, that was catching the yarn and putting it in the big cage, and that went back to the spinning, weaving place. Well I worked myself up then, I went to doffing. Our forewoman, who was always called the doffmistress, she was keeping an awful lot of bad time back and forwards, and the foreman called me out of the blue, and asked me would I do frames. It was usually elderly people that took on the frames and I said I couldn't do it, he says 'I'll learn you.' He brought me round and showed me what to do, well that was a rise in my wages, which was £3 then, and that was a big jump.

What I had to do was watch all these frames and that would be twelve frames on one side and twelve frames on the other, you see, and they spun up like a spool of thread, well you daren't let that get any fuller, and the girls had to come and lift it. So you had to keep them in rotation, so you were able to take one after the other, that they weren't all coming up at the one time, you had to work them in yourself that way. It was a wee bit difficult at the first but when I got used to it then I got settled in till I was alright, and when you get a good class of workers with you they're great.

You never got a break and the only time you knew the inspectors was coming up was that the windows was all opened and the temperature was away down, and all you could hear was, 'the inspectors must be coming the day'. They worked very, very hard for their money and they got very little for it.

*Maggie Hale, born 1920*

## Leaving School

I was fourteen in the July and my mother wouldn't let me leave school until I got a job, and I remember there was an art and craft shop in Cornmarket. My mother and I went down to apply for a job in this Cornmarket shop, it was fancy goods and that kind of thing. There was a whole queue of mothers and daughters and when my mother got in for the interview after they had talked a while she said, 'How much is the salary?' The man said, 'Two and six a week', and my mother said well she says my daughter will be more useful to be at home for two and six a week. So she wouldn't let me go for that job; well I got a job then in Apsley Street in a grocery shop and I went at half past eight in the morning to six o'clock at night, nine o'clock on Friday night and ten o'clock on Saturday night. My father used to come down and meet me coming out of work, and it was eight shillings a week.

*Margaret Mills, born 1918*

## Being a Mother

I left work when I got married in 1943 and I stayed at home then with my daughter until she went to secondary school, when she was eleven. I stayed at home and looked after the child and looked after my husband.

*Margaret Mills, born 1918*

## Opportunities for Women

When I started working, girls doing an equal job to a man would not have been paid anything like the same amount of money. I noticed it particularly when I worked in Lyon's Brothers because there I was in charge of the export office and even though it was only a small office there were three girls and myself. Our work was quite difficult because we had a lot of papers to fill in for exporting to countries all over the world, and yet the man who was in charge of the office for just home products, where it was just a question of invoicing them and sending them out without much documentation, he was paid much, much more than I was, and I really felt that that was quite an injustice. And when I went into the Civil Service where there was equal pay for equal work I really appreciated that.

When I was working in the Civil Service I got the opportunity of going to the Polytechnic for a short course to do with employment and finding people employment. Then I went on from there at night to the Polytechnic and I did a diploma in guidance and counselling, so I enjoyed doing that because it gave me the sort of taste of what university life would have been like.

I think, had I been able to choose the job that I would have liked, I would have liked to do what my daughter does now, she's a lecturer in Manchester University, she's lectured in chartered accountancy, and really that's what I would have liked to do. But I've managed in a small way to do that because I tutor an adult education course in local history. I just have an interest in local history and the education and library board approached me and asked me if I would like to do this, so I'm doing that at the moment, one night a week, and I'm enjoying that.

*Maud Meneely, born 1929*

Clive Hughes in the Merchant Navy, 1964.

## Going to Sea

When I studied and then I got into the drawing office, young people were recruited if you were doing well in your studies, you moved up into the drawing office, and of course you really became an apprentice draughtsman then. And of course that was a massive change, that was a big change because you were off the shop floor, and you really were moving kind of a blue collar up to a white collar really. I'm not saying that in any discriminatory way, I'm saying that that was just... it was a different job and the hours were slightly different really, and the work conditions were different. You had mugs and cups instead of cans in some cases. What happened was I had had a good experience when I was on the shop floor, but I joined the shipyard really to go to sea, so what happened was that I applied to the company that my brother was with, and once again that was the family influence. And the other thing about it was a lot of those firms then recruited people, brothers and that, because they knew the people were reliable in most cases, and they knew the type of people that they were recruiting. I went over for an interview on the Liverpool boat, and went there and was interviewed, they said that they would start me, and of course I finished my time on a Friday, and I started in Liverpool on a Tuesday morning.

*Clive Hughes, born 1939*

## The East Indies

Briefly I went on a marvellous trip really. I went away down round the East Indies, Borneo, Java, Sumatra, all round those ports there, and you can imagine that was still in a way the colonial age. You know, the bum boats were coming along selling stuff to the ships. There was the whole hustle, you were in ports five or six days really, going on shore at night for a drink. The next two trips I went to in actual fact were out the same route but then into Japan, and down round the Philippine Islands. At that time you had to do tickets: you had to do a second engineer's ticket and a chief engineer's ticket for promotion. You had to do sea time, a certain amount of time before you could do your ticket.

I came back to study at Belfast, to do my ticket, to do a second engineer's ticket, which I passed, at the old College of Technology again – it seemed to have played a very influential part of my life. I then wanted to get my ticket time in as quickly as possible, so I signed on for what was called 'the long jag', that was a long trip, and actually the trip lasted twenty-two months, 'cause I wanted to get all my ticket time up.

*Clive Hughes, born 1939*

## Foreign Food

The main thing with going to sea was the whole change that took place in eating habits. Remember that I'd come from Belfast, where sausages or the odd chicken was a luxury, there would be potatoes, there would be carrots, all that kind of food. I was then introduced to curry, Chinese food – because the cooks were Chinese and a lot of the men liked Chinese – we'd chop suey and all of those foods, we were introduced to all of that as well. In those days you didn't have that range of food, curry was alien to my mother and father, and in actual fact I'd heard my brother talking about curries. My brother would maybe encourage my mother to make them, but in reality we'd little knowledge of those, but I was introduced to all of those. I was introduced to all the different soups that they would have, the lot, and as I say the food was good. And of course when we then started to go ashore we would eat native food really. I mean in the Philippine Islands, a lot of it was Chinese food, the Chinese were a great influence. Then in America, the diversity of food that we came across was very good as well. Of course burgers literally were unknown over here at that time, and as we would go ashore at night, we started to eat burgers, chicken in a basket; we also used to go to Philadelphia and we used to get 'Daddy Long Legs', which were the big long chicken legs, and of course we would send out for those and get those sometimes if you fancied a change in food. It didn't matter how good the food was, you still wanted a change, you know.

*Clive Hughes, born 1939*

## Back to Normal

I got a job ashore, in a canning factory, making creamed rice and I found that very difficult to adjust with, as I found my period of coming back. I was away, my friends had moved on, and I'd been away about six or seven years, the last time for two years. My friends had moved on: they were married, they'd girlfriends, they had different relationships formed. I had not. Normally when that happened there, you would have replacement friends – other people that you met. I had no experience of that really, and I felt that it was a difficult time for me. I hadn't developed any hobbies at that time; I would say hobbies at sea were talking, chatting and working and travelling. But I hadn't developed any of those, so it was a hard year, and then I started to work in the canning factory. What then happened was I saw a job come up in the college of technology, they needed someone with a chief engineer's ticket to teach marine engineering, and in actual fact I applied for that job and got

47

it; and I really was a poacher turned gamekeeper at that time. But I moved back in and started to teach in the marine engineering section within the college of technology as it was then.

*Clive Hughes, born 1939*

## St John Ambulance

Because we were always in the background it was the ambulance crews who went to all these things, but there were times when if something happened and you were there, you were expected to just go and help.

I can remember my friend Joyce going on the scene where a young soldier was

The
St. John Ambulance Brigade

**MEMBER'S RECORD**

Lina Graham's St John Ambulance member's record book, early 1950s.

shot and her comforting him as he died and I know that she wrote to his mother afterwards. I wasn't there when it happened but I heard all about it and it was very scary, the whole thing.

We did cinema duty, I always remember I sat through *Jaws* about four times, and I was going to America that year, and was afraid to get into the water. But then we had one member of my division, she did so much duty at the Bond films and that, that I remember the attendants in the Ritz called her Pussy Galore.

There were premières in the days when Lord Wakehurst was here and I can remember one was called *Ice Cold in Alex* and all the very important people they came to the Ritz and of course we formed a guard of honour and that at the door, in uniform. We were there if anybody fell by the wayside, we were expected to pick them up.

Then we had Countess Mountbatten came over for a big dinner in the Grand Central Hotel one year and that was great. There were lots of other things – we always had a ringside seat. We went to the Agriculture Show at the King's Hall, we went to all the races.

*Lina Graham, born 1931*

## The Races

If the weather was good it was fine, but usually there was an ambulance near and you could get shelter in the ambulance. I can remember one awful one when someone came off a motor bicycle and their leg was just taken off at the boot, there was a telegraph pole with a wire coming out from it and he

Lina Graham in St John Ambulance uniform.

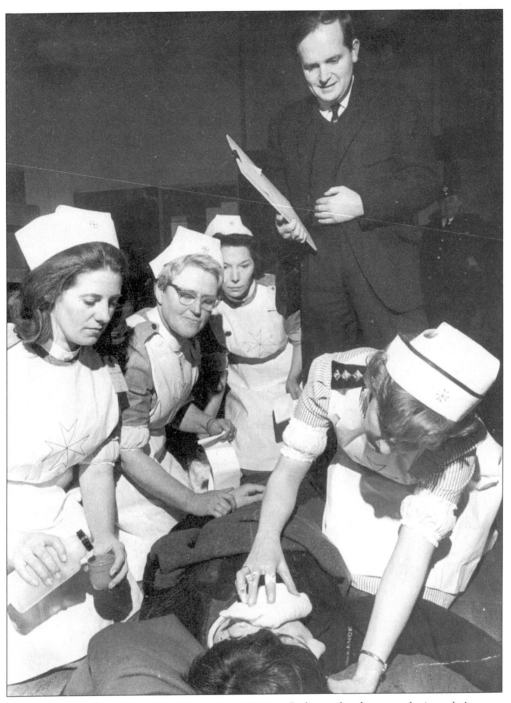

A St John Ambulance first-aid lesson in 1967. Lina Graham is bending over the 'casualty'.

hit the wire. I was quite a distance away and it was one of my members who wasn't all that long qualified. She was absolutely marvellous and she knew what to do and she lifted up the leg and put it on the stretcher with him, that was a sad one. We were always very sad when anything happened to anybody, but it was always great fun, and we always brought sandwiches and sat and ate them out in the fresh air, and it was really lovely.

Usually Dundrod and then we went to the one at Portrush as well, and there was a little man who always drove down behind us. We went down in the ambulances and he had a motorcycle and sidecar, and he used to follow us down every year. One day we braked and he didn't and then we had to get out and look after him.

At the Dundrod races all the stars were there. At one time there was car racing there and I remember all our blankets got burned trying to rescue someone from a blazing car.

*Lina Graham, born 1931*

## Football Matches

All the big football matches, we would go to them, and we really did do quite a lot of duty at the football matches, on Saturday afternoons. Mostly they were just people fainting, or if any of the players was injured, well, we would look after them but they usually had a trainer with them, who was there as well, and we would ferry them to the hospital.

There was great competition to go to them I can assure you, but it was riveting really and I mean I loved football. I found it very difficult to remember that I was still a first aider, when the football was going on. Danny Blanchflower would have been there and Pat Jennings would have been there, George Best was absolute, utter magic, he was really something, if you haven't seen him you haven't lived! Where football is concerned he was really terrific. There was such an atmosphere, I don't think there's the same atmosphere now. The atmosphere was absolutely electric when George Best was playing.

*Lina Graham, born 1931*

## First Job

Strangely enough it was in the newspaper. I got a job with the *Irish Independent* as a copy boy, I did everything and anything. This is just to show you to illustrate the advances there has been in technology: In those days nearly everything was done on the telephone, and I remember vividly going up to Stormont with a reporter, this was a Dublin paper, and he would give me the copy and I would read the copy, and I would have telephoned it through to Dublin or else take the copy down to get it sent off by the evening train to Dublin. And also on some occasions, up the Kings Hall or up to Ravenhill or up to Windsor Park with the sports reporter, and again he would be sitting watching the match, or watching the boxing, write up his copy and now and again he'd give it to me and I would dash round outside the arena, to some private house who had a

Lina Graham and her husband Wilson at a St John Ambulance ball in Belfast, 1967.

telephone, we'd made arrangements to borrow their telephone. But I'd be ringing this through to Dublin and sometimes even photographic plates, having to be taken to Dublin, taken in a train to Dublin, I think that illustrates just how much things have changed.

In the mornings I would go down to the petty sessions court to listen to what had happened the night before in Belfast. Of course it would be all minor criminal cases then. Had lunch and then in the afternoon up to Stormont to listen to our local politicians at that time. And it always seemed very trivial what was going on in Stormont, it seemed trivial to me anyway, and then as I say sporting events and whatever, it was really wonderful.

*Paddy McAteer, born 1928*

## A Hard Game

The newspaper world was a hard game and I saw it for what it was: a really tough game on the basis that these lads, at that time anyway, were on call twenty-four hours a day, and they'd no social life whatsoever. Of course there again, at that time you didn't have the staff that you would have now, a few people running a newspaper and they did everything, except photography, they always brought in a photographic. But they had a lot of responsibilities in the sense that they were on call all the time, and I didn't think that that was going to allow me to have the time to enjoy life as I would want to enjoy it. Of course even at that early stage I was thinking in terms of being out with the lads, playing football or going off

Paddy McAteer on Gobbins Path, Co. Antrim, June 1951.

enjoying life, and I didn't see a possibility of doing that and working in the newspaper world.

*Paddy McAteer, born 1928*

## Mackies During the War

I worked two shifts: a six to two and a two to ten. The six o'clock shift, I didn't like it because I got the tram at half past five and that took me to the Hippodrome and then I got another tram up the Springfield Road, to start at six o'clock. This was in munitions, I worked a lathe, that the men worked in those days, and I made nuts and parts, screws and parts for Lancaster and Stirling bombers. I really did want to join the Air Force but my mother wouldn't let me. In those days if your mother said no you accepted it, you didn't go against their wishes. So I thought this was a war effort as far as I was concerned.

*Margaret Mills, born 1918*

## Working at the Yard

Well I was placed with a man who was a fitter. His name was Hugh; his other name I never knew. He give me little tasks to perform from time to time. Luckily I was able to do these without asking too many questions because I had spent some time at the technical school doing a mechanical engineering course, so I wasn't entirely a stranger to tapping holes and that sort of thing. Simple jobs like filing, which are not simple at all of course because using a file requires quite a lot of experience and expertise, but I mean to do it at a simple level, yes there was no problem and everyone knows how to use spanners and so on. But he gave me my job, he didn't teach me, they didn't do very much of that. I have a feeling that the tradesmen, the fitters and possibly the turners also, and pattern-makers and all the rest of it, I think they rather resented the apprentices. Not on a personal level, to the extent that they would be rude to you, but I think they resented them in principle because they had suffered the deprivation of the twenties and the early thirties and they saw us as sort of

dilutees who would perhaps replace them, and I think that was the attitude, I'm fairly sure that was the case.

*William Austin, born 1926*

## The Drawing Office

Let me put it this way: when I finally hacked my way into the drawing office it was like going from hell to heaven, it really was quite wonderful. The drawing office I was in was calm, it was warm, it was civilized. You were no longer a number, you were mister, mister Austin, and the conversation which started up from time to time was very civilized and there was no stream of bad language. There was no dirt and dust and choking fumes and all the rest of it, it was wonderful being in the drawing office.

I couldn't go into a drawing office now because its all computers for the drafting, and I know nothing about that. Basically the idea of course which drives all these things would be that a good engineer needs imagination and that's the same I suppose in a lot of things. But the actual paraphernalia – well, I had to use set squares, compasses, smaller compasses called spring bows, pencils which were graded 2H, 3H and so on for hardness and rubbers and so on and do this on drawing boards. The sizes of the drawing boards had very strange names like double elephant and antiquarian, imperial half, imperial and so on; all that has disappeared for metrication. And drawing boards and set squares and so on, as far as I know they've gone and they're now computer-assisted, but it was drawing boards and drawing pins which were huge things, and it seemed to be almost criminal the damage a drawing pin inflicted at each of the four corners of a drawing board. And we used tracing paper and detailed paper and tracing linum and all sorts of things, oh it's totally different now.

*William Austin, born 1926*

## The People

They were a nice bunch and intelligent people and I found them very, very nice. The boss in the first office I was in was a keen motorcycling enthusiast and he lived in a rather large house somewhere near the old Clady Ulster Grand Prix circuit, and I like motorcycling and I'm afraid I rather played up a little in that direction in that I could always weasel out of any problem by talking motorcycles to him. I'm afraid that was a little weakness in my character.

*William Austin, born 1926*

## Post-war Years

I wasn't at Harland's for a long time after the Second World War. I left there about 1949 or '50 but I'd seen quite a lot of depletion of the merchant shipping tonnage, which caused a lot of work to be placed in the yard, and there were masses of merchant ships had to be built to replace those sunk; then they started on the big ones. But they were still building navy vessels, I mean when I was there they were still working on I think HMS *Eagle*, which was I think

perhaps a carrier in the Royal Navy at the time, and there used to be a standing joke in Harland's in the engine works anyway that if somebody didn't know what to book a job to, they would say book it to *Eagle*, and *Eagle* must have taken on its shoulders all the jobs for which they couldn't assign a number. Like a lot of other people in Harland and Wolff it was like, you may as well have been a hundred miles away, the Queens Island was an isolated place. In fact the wags used to call the engine works Stalag something or other, because you know it was guarded and you couldn't get in you couldn't get out until the whistle blew so to speak. It got worse as you worked further and further away from the city centre, until you were in your deep water wharf, you were absolutely nowhere. If you did come off the ship there was nothing to do, there was nothing there, and there wouldn't have been much in the way of transport, nobody had cars in those days, and there was a certain weariness with being trapped in the Queens Island. It wasn't an island but it might as well have been. So with other guys I suppose I was one of those who decided to get out, and I answered an ad in the *Telegraph*, I think, looking for a draughtsman for a light engineering company. I applied for and got the job, I didn't know what it was going to be, but it proved to be in the metal window industry. I spent about three years in that business and that got me round Northern Ireland quite a lot as a technical representative for this big firm in England.

There was exciting things happening in the aircraft industry and you couldn't help hearing about jet aeroplanes and so on. And Shorts at that time, 1954, they had plans to be the biggest airframe producers in the world, that was their objective, so they were recruiting a lot of people with a lot of experience, and this sounds a bit laughable but I responded to an advertisement for a draughtsman in their Efficiency department, it makes me smile. I got the job, and again I thoroughly enjoyed it, it was quite interesting to be working in Shorts. In the main factory they had a line of Canberra jet bombers lined up in various stages of building, the most distant one was complete and they were rolling them off. They were building the Britannia, the Comet, they had plans for the Belfast, the vertical take-off aircraft, the swing-wing Sherpa, experimental aircraft, quite a lot of other projects. They couldn't get space enough and they were even considering opening a drawing office in Dublin, such was the pressure on. Its hard to believe that they're now the size that it is at the moment.

*William Austin, born 1926*

## First Job

I left school when I was fourteen and my aunt got me into Milewater Mill, and I was a reeler there. I was there till the Blitz came and that part was blitzed. I was only eighteen when the war broke out. So this lady that my mother knew, she worked in Gallaher's, so when she heard that the mill..., that we were out of work, she said she would write into Gallaher's for me, and Mackies she knew somebody in Mackies, they'd started munitions there. So I said well which ever comes first I'll go, so it was the Mackies came first. By this time, I wasn't long in when we were blitzed out of Craigavad Street, and we had to go down and live in Harrisburg Street down the Shore Road. But in the meantime I was with my mother's sister in Whiteabbey, for they been blitzed out of Hogarth Street, and so my mother had said to me, 'Go you with your aunt May because she's so nervous.' But when I got there, another aunt, a sister of my father's, had taken them down to Islandmagee, to a wee country house they had. So I got into Mackies and then it was a fortune, you got about £5 or £6 then, or more, and I came up and we got the house in Harrisburg Street. We were able to be together, my father died there. So then whenever the munitions was stopping, when the war was going over, they were looking for people in Gallaher's, but they didn't want anybody that had been in the mill, you had to be out of the mill about five years. But I got into Gallaher's anyway, for I had been over five years out of the mill you see, and I worked in Gallaher's then, I was at the stripping.

*Nessie McNamee, born 1921*

## Working the Mill

The job I was at, the reeling, you could have went in at seven o'clock in the morning, like, although it didn't start until quarter past eight, but you could have turned a reel with your hand, and put cuts on the yarn. Well then there was twelve cuts on each, and then you could have took that off and started up on another new one, you see we were paid by what we done, it was piece-work, you see. But I always remember my brother, he worked in the shipyard, and he wouldn't have been up out of bed when I was leaving, and he used to shout down the stairs at me, 'Hey, Elsie, you'll be getting locked out some of these mornings!' The reeling wasn't bad, it was a bit dusty, but I wouldn't say it was a dirty job.

*Nessie McNamee, born 1921*

## Mackies

When I went in first I was in the paint spray, we done shells you know, and then I was shifted over to the aircraft part of it and I was on a wee vertical, drilling parts of the machinery for planes, and I always say that if I had have done another year, I'd have been a fully-fledged driller. You know, the way you used to have to serve five years at your trade, well I was four years, I was on a wee vertical machine they called it, and I loved it too. We done shifts, we done six to two, and two to ten, and a night shift, and when I was on the two to ten my father, dear love him, you see it was the blackout, he used to be down waiting on the trams. You had to use your brain, you had to know what you were doing like because it was for planes, and people's lives depended on it.

I think it was the Sunderland plane you called the ones that we done it for, and when you heard of them going up and all, in the war effort, it did make you feel that well you had done something, you know. I enjoyed there too, and I made good friends there, the foremen and all they were very nice and even the Mackie family were very nice men. They would have come through and had a talk and all with you.

*Nessie McNamee, born 1921*

## Gallaher's

I left Mackies on Friday night, and I started in Gallaher's on Monday morning. I didn't break any time. I was at the stripping, that was the big leaves of tobacco and you took the stem out and you made what you called wrappers, and what we sat in, we had a wee stool and it was a box and it was shaped over your knees. There was a knife in the front of it and you had like what you call two nosebags with the leaves in, and then you put the stems that you took out in another one.

*Nessie McNamee, born 1921*

## A Change of Track

I suppose it really starts with the fact that I was rather interested in natural history, snails and spiders, plants and so on. I think I had this natural curiosity as a boy, and it was never drawn out at school or anything, but I did have it, that must have been there. I was leafing through a prospectus for the old Belfast College one day, and I saw this form for a course in Applied Biology and I didn't know there was such a thing. It was part time, so I went and enrolled, and started on the first year, it was years before I got anywhere. It was three evenings a week, from half six to half nine and the subjects were botany, zoology and chemistry, and then they varied a bit – microbiology and so on. The end point of all this was that years later I had done the examinations for what is now the Royal Institute of Biology, and I had enough technical knowledge to get a job that was advertised in the biology section of the forensic science laboratory in Verner Street as it was at the time. They wanted me because I had some knowledge of photography and I had done some technical illustration in Shorts which I was able to show them. They had as part of their brief the education of the police and they were going to move to the new laboratory in Newtownbreda. They would have an exhibition and teaching area, and they really wanted me to get involved in that as well as doing bench-work in the biology section.

*William Austin, born 1926*

## Interest in Biology

The sea shore was rather an interesting place to me, and the things that most people would walk past, I can remember thinking about and wondering about the various seaweeds and so on. And having started to study biology at the old college of technology, this featured a lot. We had to go down every year to the marine biology station at Portaferry, and spend a week there, and we had to go across to London. But I learned about the seaweed that there was: the browns and the reds, according to where you were you got certain seaweeds growing, and no matter where you were round the British Isles you would still get the same seaweeds.

*William Austin, born 1926*

## Forensic Work

In the laboratory as a whole, prior to the Troubles certain people were asked to undertake certain things which fitted into no particular category. For example, fires: it could have been a biologist or a forensic biologist or forensic chemist – those were the two breeds by the way – it could have been either that handled that. But when the Troubles started then there was a great swelling in the numbers of people to match the incidents, the trouble in the streets and weapons being brought to the laboratory for proving, and the determination of what caused the fire, whether it was malicious, whether the premises where firebombed or whether it was an accident or whatever, because all this had to be done for insurance purposes. So at the start we all had to muck in: in certain areas, for example I wouldn't have had any knowledge of weapons, but there were a few guys who happened to like looking at firearms and they were able to do that.

But I can remember searching. There was a large furniture shop in Arthur Street I think, Hannah and Brownes, and they were at the toffee-nose side of the market. Their place was burned out, and I remember five or six bins of charred material were brought from the seat of the fire; that is where the most intense burning had occurred.

William Austin at work in the forensic lab.

It's hard to believe this, but it was in the fifth bin, near the bottom, that I found what I was looking for, evidence of an incendiary device. But all that stuff had to be examined, and very carefully, before that was discovered.

The biologist would have been looking at the clothing of persons who were injured or deceased, but I had made a transfer, just about the time of the start of the Troubles. I had done some of the work, in fact one of the first of the bombings occurred at the Tomb Eel Fisheries and I remember one of the bits that was brought to the laboratory by the police was the remains of an alarm clock, which had clearly been used in a timing device. So any material, we had to look at it and try to find out where it came from, if we could find out where that clock came from, there was a chance that we could narrow it down to where it was bought in Northern Ireland. So I started to pad around the streets of the centre of Belfast going from jeweller to jeweller asking about this clock, I didn't make any secret of the fact, I told them where I was from and the objective of my enquiries. One of them obviously became suspicious about this and telephoned the police and this caused consternation in Musgrave Street police station, as I subsequently learned and they despatched two detectives to the shop that I'd been in. The funniest thing was that I was crossing Donegall Place on a pedestrian crossing and I met these two detectives and I knew them and we wished each other good morning, and they were looking for me as the possible criminal or terrorist or

whatever! I think that caused quite a lot of consternation for a while, but I was involved a little.

*William Austin, born 1926*

## Questioned Document Examination

I transferred at my own request because I rather liked the work into an area of the forensic sciences known as questioned document examination, this dealt with the examination of hand writing, typewriting paper, alterations to documents and anything to do with documents. I found it rather fascinating and I got on very well with the guy that was doing it, and he was rather desperate for someone to come and help him, so I moved into the area of questioned documents.

If you write on a writing pad to a holiday destination you want a brochure or to know about the place. So you send this letter off and you've used a ballpoint pen say, the underlying sheet will carry an indentation of your writing, now you might be able to see that indentation if you are heavy-handed with the pen, but even if you aren't the indentation will be there. Now two rather clever guys in England, Bob Foster and Doug Freeman, they devised a piece of equipment that could very often demonstrate that indented writing. You see what would happen, on the next sheet, the sheet bearing the indented writing, you would then perhaps if you were an ill-intentioned person, you may write an abusive anonymous letter, or a threatening letter to someone. So the letter that they received would be bearing indentations of your earlier writing which was an overt writing in which you would have your address in the conventional place, and an opening salutation, the text and then a concluding endearment of some kind, and if we could pick up any of those, it's possible that the police could have been knocking at your door.

Before that apparatus was devised it was a matter of using shallow light, at a very shallow angle and turning the document relative to the light, and surprising results could be obtained by that method.

ESDA is electrostatic detection apparatus and it came into prominence in certain trials I think to do with terrorist cases. It got into the national press and the term 'ESDA examination' I think became known, certainly to crime reporters and quite a few readers. It had been in use for some years before that.

You became aware that a person who was seemingly awful nice and well matured and developed, could be guilty of some pretty awful things, and the way you saw this was, after having worked at material you may have had to go into court to give evidence, and the person was sitting in the courtroom, and this was your first glimpse of that man or woman, and quite a lot of them looked surprisingly normal and ordinary. I can remember people saying of the Yorkshire Ripper, you would know he was evil and I can't agree with that. I think if you'd passed that man Peter Sutcliffe in the street, you wouldn't give him a second glance, you wouldn't have believed him capable of the things that he did. So I

suppose there was a certain amount of that: that you became rather more prepared to accept things. In the words of one of my colleagues, he used to say, 'There are boys for everything.' There were people for everything, you just wouldn't know.

*William Austin, born 1926*

## Money and the Shipyard

By the time I was there, there were about 17,000 men worked in it, and the interesting thing about it was that to start with there were shops, men ran shops within the yard, where you could buy tobacco or cigarettes, you could buy sweets, you could buy various things like that. Now they were not official but they would run them from their lockers, and there would be some of them more entrepreneurial men, who would in actual fact run these wee shops and sell stuff. And of course, remember that some of them were giving stuff on tick as well. So there was credit being given, and maybe quite a sizeable payback on pay day for some of the men who weren't so sensible with their money. There was of course some gambling associated with it as well, pitch and toss, and various games like that. Maybe it was a tragedy, losing their pay so easily. And the other interesting thing about it was that there was quite an evangelical movement within the shipyard, at that time, which a lot of people didn't really seem to know about. I remember there was an all-male society; there were girls worked in the offices, but the offices was remote to me, out in the shop floor. I mean, I didn't really move into an office situation till after I had about four years served of my time. There was this evangelical movement, and there would be a lot of people be brought in for to run services and that over the lunch-break and some of those would be quite big services. You moved every six months on to work with a different person, to give you experience. It was quite a good system. The man that I worked with to start with had no interest in that, but the second man, he in actual fact was a chap called Archie Holmes, and I'm still friendly with Archie Holmes, and he was a fine chap, very decent. He never wanted to put his ideas down your throat really, but he was very kind, very caring and he was interested in the services, and I would go with him to those as well.

*Clive Hughes, born 1939*

## Teacher Training

There was no other place where teachers could be trained, there was no training college in Belfast at first, but there was at the end of my training career, at the end of my two years, when I came back, Stranmillis had started. I went straight to Marlborough Hall in Dublin and we spent the first term there, and a the end of that term we were told we had to go back home, because the military had taken over Marlborough Hall, and we must get out. So we were sent home just with our... you might say with our handbag, and we were told that they'd be in touch with us, when we could come back. So I suppose it was about a month we were home, before word came from them to say to come back. We were stationed then in Harcourt Street Hotel, and that's where we spent the rest of the time. We travelled down into the town for lectures and that sort of thing, and back up to the hotel for meals and slept there.

*Lena Purdy, born 1901*

## First Day as a Teacher

I remember my first day going up the street, nobody spoke to me, and I wondered what sort of place I'd come to. I said well tomorrow morning I'm going to speak to everybody and see how this goes down. So the next morning I said 'good morning, good morning everybody' – I had them in the whole of my hand, and we just took to each other right away.

It wasn't a school at all – it was just a place upstairs, you know a building, they called it the school. There was the master here, he was Mr Helan from Ballynahinch, and on the other side there was Miss Webb from Portadown, and I was the one in the middle. It was very difficult to teach young children with the master here, and an assistant here, but there was a funny side to it too. Down below there was a kind of a place, there was a store there, and the floor in Miss Webb's end of the school, was what we called the gallery, it was seated up like a theatre, and with age you see the knots in the wood fell out and there was a hole there. And sometimes a mouse would come up and the children would shout 'Please teacher, a mouse!' and she would get up and hold her skirts, standing on a chair, but many times there wasn't a mouse at all. The children did this for fun, because they liked to see her jumping onto the chair and standing up, you know what children are.

*Lena Purdy, born 1901*

## Travelling to Work

I travelled from Glengormley. I got up early and I got a trolleybus at that time, down in. It would then take me into Bridge Street, so I would get off there and then I would walk down to the shipyard. Sometimes I got an Ulsterbus, but of course I was in the lucky position that I could get a trolley bus or an Ulsterbus, and then I would walk down to the shipyard, sometimes along the old coal quays, sometimes back up over the Queens Bridge. Of course you would be passing the horses there tethered up, because they would have had trace horses to help the carts to go up over the steep incline at the bridge, and the old horse would be there with us, feedbag on, even at that time of the morning sometimes.

*Clive Hughes, born 1939*

## Wartime WVS

I started a WVS in Crossgar at that time, and then I went on to organize in 1948 the first WI. As a matter of fact they just recently they celebrated their fiftieth anniversary and that kept me busy. I was an ARP warden, my husband was the captain or whatever you'd like to call it.

I drove the ambulances for practices and actually the night we took over the ambulance I drove from Belfast, and I'd never driven a big vehicle except a tractor up to then. The boy that was with me said, 'Do you know what you're driving at, you're doing about fifty! Slow down a bit!' he said, so of course I slowed down. But I got home safely anyway, but it was an awful experience, I thought I would never get home.

Part of the work was looking after the evacuees. We had some from Gibraltar, it was a Gibraltarians' camp, organized at Newcastle, and I was in charge of the clothing. Now while they were very nice people, most of them, one or two were just a wee bit – you know – they were grabby. If you gave them something nice to wear they didn't appreciate it, they would want something else. But on the whole they were all right, and I used to go there once a week to look after them.

*Lena Purdy, born 1901*

## Wearing Trousers

Driving a tractor in a field one autumn, I wore trousers, and people didn't like that, they said that trousers were for men, they weren't for ladies. However my husband was short of a hand, and they were cutting corn, so I got on the tractor with John's hat and trousers, and drove the tractor up and down to save a man. There was somebody waiting on a bus, there was a bus stop just beside the field, and this man yells over, 'Hey John, that's a good looking fella you have this morning! Where did you get him?'

*Lena Purdy, born 1901*

Sheila Hughes in 1945.

## Treading the Boards

You see the thing is my father didn't seem to think it very important that I had a great education. Now he sent my brother to the Belfast Royal Academy, but I didn't start school till I was seven, and I went to the Girls' Model School for a couple of years, and then the war broke out and I went away with Fossett's Circus. I travelled all round Ireland in Fossett's Circus for a while and then I came back again, and I went to Bloomfield Collegiate School, which was evacuated out to Glenariff. I went there in 1941 for two years, and then it was just about my fifteenth birthday in September of 1943, when I left and went straight into the theatre as a dancer.

I was nine when I was with Fossett's Circus, and it was really great because it was during the war you see and there was no petrol for them to move from place to place, so of course it was all by horse drawn wagon. You know, I used to have to get up at some unearthly hour, about five in the mornings, and move from one little town to another, so that was quite thrilling as well.

I just went there because my parents knew the Fossetts who owned the circus, but I mean I used to be taught all sorts of things. I was taught how to walk a tightrope and I used to... sometimes I did go on to assist a magician who was there, a chap called Jung Lin Sem, he called himself. I don't know what his real name was. But I assisted him and was able to ride the horses and all sorts of things like that. There was an elephant there, a lovely little elephant called Nica, and she was only quite a baby really, and

Mrs Fossett used to take her on. I remember Nica would never go on unless she had her pound of caramels which were in the bag. Papers and all, wrappers and everything, all were posted into Nica's mouth and she ate those before she went on, you know. But that was a lovely time as well, although I missed of course being at home, but my mother used to come and visit me every so often you know, if we were anywhere near. But it was just to be evacuated away from here during the war.

I did say to you that I didn't go to school very much really, and I was moved around from place to place but I suppose you could call it the 'university of life' – I don't know. But I didn't go to school very much at all. Just before I went away with the circus I was at the Model but then I was evacuated first of all to Newcastle, that was just after the first bombing raid on Belfast. It was just incendiary bombs, and I can remember coming home from the Empire with my mother and father in the car, although I was very young, and I can remember coming through that air raid, and it was a very frightening experience. And then I was evacuated immediately to Newcastle in County Down. I remember so well seeing the planes coming over because they came over, the German planes, from the south of Ireland and passed Newcastle, and I can remember seeing the sky lit up in Belfast, and knowing that my parents and my brother were there, it was a terrifying experience, you know. And luckily they were alright, but I then went to another school in Newcastle, and we did nothing but dig for victory, grow onions and all those

The finale of a performance at the Empire Theatre, Belfast, in 1946.

sort of things, you know. That's what I did, and then I went to Bloomfield Collegiate which was as I told you evacuated to Glenariff.

*Sheila Hughes, born 1928*

## Job in the Theatre

I was just fifteen I finished my formal schooling and I might tell you I really would never survive these days if I wanted to get a job, because I didn't go in for any exams or pass any exams, you know I really came out of school with no qualifications whatsoever. But I went straight into the theatre, and it was a very very nice atmosphere, it was what I had always wanted to do, so I was very lucky in that I was able to do that, and all the company were so friendly and we were working together, you see, for so many years. And there were some marriages within the company as well, we really all got to know one another very very well. A lot of the girls where from the south of Ireland from Dublin mostly, and they stayed in digs up here, the landladies were all wonderful to them, you know theatrical landladies are really quite something apart, and they're more like mothers than anything else you know and they looked after the girls so very, very well.

*Sheila Hughes, born 1928*

## Thrown into a Grown-up World

I was, I suppose, thrown into a grown-up world, and sometimes we used to work cabarets; well my mother always came with us as a chaperone, always, because we used to go into the army camps and things like that. And of course four young girls, we used to go out in fours as dancers, you know there would be some other members of the show would come as well to do their act, but when it was dances there was just four of us would go at a time. And my mother always came with us because we were all very young, you know really, and I suppose it was felt that we had to be kept a good eye on. So we were thrown into that world, and also now I have girlfriends, one in particular who I've had since I was a tiny, tiny child, and she is still my friend, and over all those years, I still kept very friendly with her and my other friends. But then you see we were working whenever they were off, and vice versa, so it was difficult in a way, although we did keep friends.

*Sheila Hughes, born 1928*

## Behind the Scenes

You see, going from live, then they started recording, and I remember in Limegrove you see people enjoyed that then, because if they did something wrong it could be you repeated and so on, and so forth. I remember Mrs Roosevelt, you know Franklin Roosevelt's wife, she came – that was when I was in the BBC – and she was lovely. It was one night and she was going to do a chat at someplace, but before that she was going to do a television interview and I had to make her up before she went to do the talk, and then she was coming back to the studios. She was absolutely lovely, but she was so nervous she kept running to the toilet. So I'd get a little bit of make-up on, then she'd have to go backwards and forwards, but she was an absolutely delightful person. You remember people like that, and people like the Aga Khan, the old Aga Khan, who used to get weighed, do you remember with gold on one side and so on, and he was so big, I could hardly get him into the chair, you know, he was enormous. But that sort of thing was fascinating, and then people like Arthur Askey, oh Arthur was lovely bless his heart, he was a lovely man, and I did a lot of shows with him, with Benny Hill, and so on and so forth. You go through them all you know, but I can't remember – I mean there was so many of them, you know, it just was fabulous.

When I became head of the department, one had to have make-up trainees, but you'd have to find people who had an artistic ability, but apart from that, they were good with people and they were good at mixing. Now I

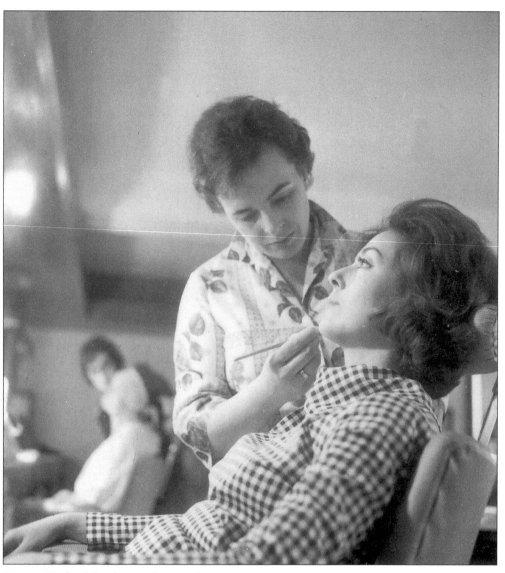

Maureen Orchard-Smith at work as a make-up artist.

got a girl once who was a very good make-up artist but her personality was against her, so I had to let her go, and then another girl, who'd a lovely personality but hadn't got the artistic ability, you've got to try and combine you know: very, very difficult.

I remember once when I became head of the department and we were doing a series with Tom Jones, and Engelbert Humperdink. One week it was Tom Jones, next week Engelbert Humperdink, and in the studio, Shirley Bassey was doing a show, well it was Tom Jones' show, but she was the star, you know. But life became very difficult so the producer in the end decided she would have to go, because she was being very difficult and very rude. So he told her to go out of the studio which she did, but in the corridor there were pictures of Tom all along, because it was his show, it was all his shows, so there were all these pictures of Tom, so what did she do? Write rude words over all the pictures right along the corridor! I went into the main make-up room and Tom was there being made up, and he said, 'And I thought she liked me'. We never used Shirley Bassey again, Lew Grade said no, he was the boss then. He said 'no, won't use her again', so we didn't. She maybe did for other companies but not for him, because it was really too much: you can take so much, and then there's a feeling that we're not going to have it.

At first when I went into it, you went in and you thought, you were a little bit in awe of people, but then they were just people, and they all had their worries their troubles and everything, and you'd listen and you know, it just was, it didn't mean anything in the end.

It's funny because I met so many people like Ella Fitzgerald who was a fabulous person. She said, 'Do you mind if I stand up, because these corsets are killing me if I sit down?' She was fabulous, you know: she really was. And you just think, oh that's lovely, Sophie Tucker. Now Peter Lawford I don't know whether you remember him, he was married to Patricia Kennedy. Now we did a big show, for six times, and we had Peggy Lee and Joe Stafford and all big artists coming in. And Peter Lawford was one of them, and I had him, because I'd to do changes on him, he was wearing helmets and various things and everything, and we were talking while we were sitting, he was very nervous. And we were talking away about things, and I said, 'You know, Mr Lawford, I thought you were so good in *Little Women*, with Katherine Hepburn', and he said, 'That was before the war, I was in the one with Elizabeth Taylor after the war.' I thought, 'Oh help!' but he was very nice about it. And then we had Benny Hill, and Harry Secombe who I adore, he was lovely, he was lovely indeed. One time we were having a bit of trouble on the Joe Stafford show, and Benny Hill was on, and I said – I'd known him of old – and I said, 'Benny, there's a bit of an atmosphere. If you can help...' And he was very good, he did his best to try and make the atmosphere a little bit better. And then we'd people like Claire Bloom who was difficult. You got so many artists who were difficult and you had to cope with them, because some of my make-up artists sometimes were in tears trying to cope with the way some of them behaved. It was difficult to deal with some of them, I can assure you. I

Maureen Orchard-Smith at work as a make-up artist.

just got mad once or twice, with Zsa Zsa Gabor, who didn't want anyone to make her up, and I took the make-up stuff into her and she threw it all about the room, and I thought 'oh yes', and she just told me her life story. She didn't want to know about my doing any make-up; she was going to do it all and everything, except in the evening she wanted her neck done, because her neck was too light you know, and she wanted some make-up on her body. Well by the time I'd finished talking to her, and she didn't want to know about me, I went out of the room, and I met Hattie Jaques who was a lovely person, and I starting to cry with rage. Hattie was very good – 'Don't you worry, my love' – and all that, and she was very nice. And I went upstairs and that night, I'd to come down and put this body make-up on, that was one thing Zsa Zsa Gabor couldn't do herself. So instead of taking hot water I took cold water and the pancake, and I got my own back, because she yelled, so I felt much better, you know. But you do get tempers and everything; not a lot though, and most of the tempers came from people who weren't really stars. If you got the stars we had – Laurence Olivier in a play, Ralph Richardson and people like that – they were fabulous because they knew their job, they were professional. It was some of the people who thought they were stars who were temperamental you know.

Harry Secombe was one, because he was always bright and breezy and he came in to do the Joe Stafford show and he didn't want to do it, it just was not his sort of thing. So what he did he went round all the technicians – everybody – and handed out five-pound notes. He said they might as well have it because he didn't want to do the show. He was very good, and then now, who else would I say? Benny Hill: I was very fond of Benny because I remember once I met him outside and I was waiting for someone and this person was late, and he was so good because he stayed with me and waited until the person came. And I enjoyed working on his shows. In BBC days they were quite different than what he did later you know, and I enjoyed those because we did rehearsals in his flat, and so on. I sort of knew he was a very lonely person in a way, but he loved going to Paris because he loved the food and everything. I liked him very much indeed. There are some people that you do grow fond of, but, you know, other people you don't want to see again, ever.

*Maureen Orchard-Smith, born 1924*

## Life After the BBC

I finished in the Seventies, it was about 1971. Well I was married and I and my husband, we'd been across here, and he thought it would be a good idea to come over here to live and he thought to take up doing a bed and breakfast sort of thing over here, you know. Anyway it was a bit of a decision, I wasn't entirely happy about it, but we thought we'll come over and we found somewhere at Limavady. But we gave it up, and really we only lasted a year, because, that's right, it was 1971, and there were all the Troubles, and when you're over in London you didn't realize how bad the situation was over here, you see. And you just didn't know, and of course it wasn't a good year to start, I mean in time it would have been alright, but it just was very bad, it all finished you know.

*Maureen Orchard-Smith, born 1924*

## Further Education

What happened was that I had really decided that I wanted to go to sea as well. And I was introduced to another massive influence in the industrial life and that was further education. And I'm not honestly sure that the full significance of that hasn't been understood, in the wider community. University degree work – some people had the opportunity to go, and I ultimately did have the opportunity but unfortunately couldn't avail myself of that opportunity. But further education then took a lot of people like myself up into levels of study and enabled us to study, and from this point of view it was a massive way of enabling people to progress and go on within a work situation, while still working, and going at nights. To start with I had to go four nights a week to the Tech as it was called then, and then there were trade scholarships which were available, where you had a reduction in your money, but the government paid you a certain amount. I remember the first one I went on I was cut £5 a week, but my mother and father were very supportive of that, because they're country people and they respected education, and they knew that education was the way forward. Maybe I was encouraged by recognizing that I didn't want to work in the shipyard all

my life, that in actual fact I wanted to move on and I wanted to work in a different environment as well. I was doing mechanical engineering, there weren't the same range of specialized courses that there are now, it was the old national certificate and higher national certificates which were there.

*Clive Hughes, born 1939*

## The Labour Exchange

My introduction to the Labour Exchange was when I reported for duty there, as I arrived to take up my duties. I saw a crowd outside, a lot of policemen and a large number of the great unemployed, who had chained themselves to the railings in protest against the treatment. Large placards saying 'We want work or bread' – this wasn't so long after the famous Giro hunger marches on London. It was a very depressed time. And the work dealing with the unemployed was depressing, because we had no work to offer them each day that they came to sign on. They signed on in those days three times a week on Monday, Wednesday and a Friday, and on Friday they got paid. Each time they would say 'Any work?' and we would say 'Nothing doing', and that went on and you can imagine it was depressing to me, to see men old enough to be my father in such dire straits. The amount of benefit they got was small, a single man got 17s a week, if he was married he got an extra 10s for his wife, and for each child 3s. So a married man with one child got 30s a week which was exactly what I was being paid. And there seemed little prospect of finding work for them, but people who were in and out most often were dockers, who of course were employed in a very casual way: they reported each morning to the docks, and there was either a ship to be off-loaded or loaded, or there was not. And even amongst them, even if there was a ship to be off-loaded, it was a matter for the foreman, or ganger to pick his team. They were then allowed to come back to the labour exchange and sign on as having had no work that day, or sign off again. That went on really until the summer of 1939 and, as I say, the war clouds were gathering. There were all sorts of signs of preparation, gas masks were issued, the office staff had formed themselves into an ARP team. I became the gas expert, having done two days of a gas course. And I can still recall the delight when, one morning in August, my supervisor came to me and he said, 'When your men come in to sign on today' – these were all general labourers – 'when they come in to sign today, ask each one has he got his own pick and shovel, and if he has send him round to me, because we'll have a job for them.' This was the first time when we really were able to offer employment to these men. Employment of course consisted of digging trenches and making air raid shelters in the parks in London, filling sandbags and shoring the place up. There was this mixture of feelings that here we were on the brink of war, which was quite obviously going to come, and yet there was the bonus of employment.

*William Wright, born 1921*

## Computer Course

The computing I found very confusing for about two months: there were that many new terms, records and bits and bytes and files. There was so much words, addresses, all being thrown at you and I thought for the first two months 'I'm not going to be able to cope with this', and then suddenly it all started clicking into place, and I must say I thoroughly enjoyed the two years of that course.

I don't think I foresaw anything like the PCs as they are now, but you did imagine that machines would get faster and bigger in the sense of being able to do more. I don't think anybody envisaged the sort of miniaturization that we have now. Its easy to see how it came about looking back on it, but then what you've got to remember is in the late sixties, early seventies the hardware was the expensive bit. If you were a bank and you were going to buy a computer you were going to pay millions of pounds for it, and your staff to run it were only going to cost you hundreds each, or maybe a thousand, fifteen hundred as a yearly salary. So all the money went into the hardware and the people were an incidental. I mean, it's completely changed now, the hardware is very cheap and the people are very expensive.

*Ruth McAllister, born 1951*

## Early Computers

I could have gone to university and done a degree, if I wanted to, but I decided to look for a job, and I started as a programmer with a company called ICS computing, in 1971. Started work there and I stayed with them for the next twenty years, in one shape or form, the company changed its name, and I changed my job, quite a variety of times. That was commercial computing: they were a software house who were running what is called bureau service, they were developing software and running it on their own computer, but the software was developed on behalf of other companies, and run centrally for them. Everything, payrolls, a lot of accounts, because in those days you couldn't go out and buy an accounting package – you had to write your own. So it was only bigger companies who could afford to pay for software to be written specifically for them that made use of computing. Working for that company I saw it right through. When hardware started to come less expensive, smaller companies could afford to buy their own mini-computers, again generally speaking still having to pay for software to be written for them or having to buy packages to run them. The packages would have cost thousands of pounds, not the hundreds or few hundreds that we're used to today. That was very interesting because I was then starting to go out and move around, meet people from other companies: you go out to the clients' sites to load the software up, discuss the software design with them. I've always worked for organizations which are doing work on behalf of external clients. I have never worked in a software or computing department, which was just one department in another company.

When I started in '71, we were working with one mainframe, an ICL 1901 which was kept in a special room with a suspended ceiling, suspended floor, air conditioning and special people, computer operators, to operate it. When I left, everybody was working on PCs and mini-computers which could have sat in the corner of the office and worked off a thirteen amp plug. You know, it had changed completely, but you still had to write software. The equipment and the facilities you were using had changed a lot, but when it comes right down to it, a lot of the techniques used to write code are still very much the same.

*Ruth McAllister, born 1951*

# CHAPTER 3
## *Relationships and marriage*

Margaret Mills and her husband in
Hogarth Street, 1955.

Margaret Mills's wedding day in 1943.

## Billy Mills

There were quite a lot of boys in the neighbourhood, you know the boys we went to school with and that. But my mother took a cottage out near Saintfield. I was fifteen at the time and my sister was eleven and a half. It was a cottage on a corner, the month of August she took it for. All the boys of the countryside used to gather at that corner, and they would have played marbles and that kind of thing. This boy Billy Mills, he took a notion to me and I was fifteen and he was seventeen and he took a notion to me then. We were just friends for a long time and played

marbles and talked and that kind of thing. But he asked me if I would go with him out to a motor race, there was a motor race that went round by Comber and Newtownards then, and he asked me if I would go with him. I said, 'I'll have to ask my mother', so I said to my mother and she says, 'Well, you can go if you take Olive with you', this was my sister. So we took Olive with us to the motor race at Comber, Newtownards. We went in a bus to Saintfield and then we got another bus out to Comber. The only thing was we were at the race and we went in for tea and that, but my sister and I, we were so quiet and so bashful, we needed to go to the toilet and we didn't like to say, and it sort of spoiled the day for us.

*Margaret Mills, born 1918*

## First Husband

He was a farmer and I was staying in a farm with a family called Stewart, and I think she took me in merely because her husband had died recently and she had a baby boy. I think she thought that I would be company, and maybe help her with the family. He lived just up in the farm beside us. I had lots of other boyfriends, but nothing serious, but however we got married, and we lived in his old home which belonged to his father, and it needed a lot of fixing up, do you know. So I kept on teaching and I think I was, I'm not boasting when I say this, I think I was a pretty good farmer's wife, because I was brought up on the farm.

*Lena Purdy, born 1901*

William Hutton with his wife and twin daughters, 1952.

## Married Life

My brother introduced us, and shortly after that we started going out together. I was only sixteen then, and I was married when I was twenty-one and one month, so I was over four years going with David before we got married.

He was a motor mechanic, and he was working as a motor mechanic at that time. Then, in those early thirties, business wasn't very good and he went across to Cambridge to work. He was with a firm over there, I think it was the British Rock Team company, they called it. They used to clear buildings of vermin, and David went over and worked with them, for a while. Well then he came back to Belfast, that was before we were married of course, he came back to Belfast and he started working. He was looking after the fleet of motors and vans belonging to the Maypole Dairy company which is extinct now. And then later on, after that, he started to work in the Belfast Co-op dairy, in Frederick Street; he was working on the machinery, in the dairy. In fact he was there until he died in 1965; it was about, I think, about twenty-two years he worked in the Co-op.

David was a very steady-going person and I got very fond of him and we were married in October, although it was more or less against the wishes of my mother. She didn't think I was old enough to get married, although I was

William Hutton and family at Ballindrum, Moneymore, in 1952.

twenty-one, and she just didn't – she wasn't married until she was much older than that. And she thought I was much too young to get married, but we got married anyhow. And we were married in York Street, we went up to Portrush for our meal, and then we came back and went on the boat to Scotland, went over to Scotland for a few days. When we came back and we actually hadn't a house of our own at the time, we had a part house. An old lady friend of another friend of ours was living by herself, and she let us part of the house. And we stayed in it for nearly a year, before they built houses then up in Torrens Avenue, off the top of the Oldpark Road, up near Cliftonville Circus. And we got a new house there, and we were in it from 1936 till Hitler blitzed us out of it in 1941. We were about five years in Torrens Avenue, and that was the time that we went to Hillsborough, for my brother had got the house from the farmer.

*Ruby Purdy, born 1914*

## Husband's Illness

David, when he was a child, when he was young, he smoked quite a lot, because his mother died when he was only about thirteen or fourteen years of age. And the father had a grocery business where they sold cigarettes, and of course he used to go in and get cigarettes in the shop. And they got him – he was a very heavy smoker, and he actually got bronchitis, but whether that was the cigarettes or not... for his mother she had been slightly bronchial too. Although she died in the big flu of 1918, that's what killed her, David was always troubled with his chest, and there was times when he used to be with the doctor who lived two doors above us, Doctor Emerson. And there was one day my sister went into the doctor's and David was just gone out in front of her. Emerson knew who my sister was, or knew it was my sister, and he says 'There's a man and he will not take time off work, he says he's anxious to get back to work', and he says he's not fit to go back to work. But David insisted in coming off, he'd been on the sick this time, but the bronchitis used to get him, he was ill every winter, he was always off for a certain amount of time. But that particular time, he took so bad: it was 1959, on the Monday morning, I remembered it now, the 5th of January 1959, just after David Bleakley's election, when he had lost the seat.

*Ruby Purdy, born 1914*

## Widowhood

Actually when David died, the three older boys they were all married, and George was up in Kinawley. He talked to me that he'd like to be nearer Belfast, because I was just at home with Michael, who was only twelve, just barely twelve, when David died. So George put in to get a transfer nearer Belfast, and got Newtownards. Well I decided that the house was too big for Michael and I to stay in it. Well George and Alma came up and stayed with me, after he got to Newtownards, until they would get a house to stay in, they stayed with us. Well then I sold the house, and it was only a few months, about the

Lina Graham and her friend Betty Pollock on the way to a ball in Enniskillen, early 1950s.

month of April or May it was sold, and that was four or five months after David died, and then we went to live with a nephew, Michael and I. We were there for about thirteen months when we got the flat. But I had never been out doing anything outside the house, as far as work was concerned, until David died. And I went then and looked for something to work at, so I got back into doing office work, which I had been used to doing. And then after thirteen months we got the flat up in Kilbroney, and Michael and I moved up there. We were there for about four years, until I got this flat here in Woodstock House. But I kept on working and I was involved in different things in the Labour Party, and that kind of thing. And we had actually started the East Belfast Historical Society, it was commenced in the Labour Hall, in Cheviot Avenue, the hall which my husband had helped to gather up the money for, to buy it, years before, although the hall wasn't bought until after he died. We worked at all sorts of things like that, the Labour Party and the church was very much in my mind. I'd always belonged to the church, but with the family being smaller and everything, I didn't always get the opportunity of doing so much in the church, as it was away on the Lisburn Road and it wasn't just beside, it wasn't convenient always to get over to the things through the night when the family were at home. But then when I was on my own with Michael, Michael was able to stay with friends, and I got involved with the bowling club, which we only started for women at that time. There had been a bowling club for the men, for years before it, but there never

had been anything for the women, they didn't want the women in the club at all. But we thought it wasn't fair that we didn't get playing, so we played on a different night, the men played on Friday nights and we played on Monday nights. Well then the men's club it dwindled away so much that they were closing up and they'd started coming to the women's club, and we had quite a good club for quite a while. The trouble was a lot of our people got older and weren't able to come, and quite a number of them had died, and that sort of put paid to the bowling club.

I expect that's what it was because I always liked plenty of company and I like to get involved in different things. Because when we were in York Street, there was the swimming club, although I didn't learn to swim really. We had that and the dramatic society and the social club, and the guild, and all those sort of things belonging to the church. And Sunday school: I never taught in Sunday school. My sister did, but I was always involved in other things. Although I was always very fond of church, I didn't like missing it; I didn't feel my day was right unless I was there.

*Ruby Purdy, born 1914*

## Loneliness

I think the main thing is nobody prepares you for the loneliness. I mean you can go out, and I'm out a lot and that's fine, but I mean in the end you come in to go to bed and that's it, or you come in the evening and sit down, and you suddenly realize.... I just realized some months after Jim died, that here am I and I've never lived alone until I was almost seventy-four. I find myself if I haven't been out maybe for a few nights and somebody comes in I feel I'm talking too much, you know I feel I have to apologize for talking too much.

*Peg Armstrong, born 1919*

## Marriage

I met my husband-to-be at a dance actually, whenever I was there one evening. The way we were off, you know if we were off we used to go to dances, and all that sort of thing. And I met him at a dance, and our relationship grew from there.

I remember my wedding day, yes. I made my own wedding dress, because although we were married in 1951, and

Lina Graham with friend Violet and dog Chico at Ballinamallard, early 1950s.

the war finished in '45, there was still very difficult times, and I went down to Dublin to get the material for my dress, and I made it all myself. There wasn't really a great deal, even then, and I can remember we had a reception, we were married at St Peter's on the Antrim Road, and we had our reception in the Belfast Castle.

*Sheila Hughes, born 1928*

## Meeting My Wife

We met at the Craigantlet Hill Climb, my cousin and myself had gone to watch the races there and amongst the spectators we saw two rather glamorous young ladies, and decided to try and make their acquaintance. We started to chat and walked home, made arrangements to go to the pictures and from then on, we were, as it were, semi-walking out together. There were other girls in my life and other fellows in hers at the time, but it didn't last very long, because as I say I went to London, and we were parted. I think that the only contact we had was Valentine's Day and cards were exchanged. And then of course I came into the Air Force and when I got my first leave, we met up and went to the cinema quite a lot.

*William Wright, born 1921*

## Wedding Day

I'd been granted this extended leave when I came home; this was to make up for all the leave I hadn't had for four years. And so we decided to get married

in December. I'd come home at the end of October, and I'd been told that my leave would be at least a month. So we made all our plans. Now although the war was over there was still an awful lot of austerity about the place, but by pulling a few strings here and there, we were able to organize an iced wedding cake, Gay had saved a lot of clothing coupons, and had a white wedding which was quite unusual then. And the wedding took place in St Anne's Cathedral in Belfast. It was all planned, as they say, when I received a telegram from the ministry to say that my leave was now considered to be ended and I was to report to Aldergrove – well at least it was Northern Ireland. I went up there, and found that it was virtually a transit camp, although I had a few duties to do – sat on a couple of court marshals and courts of inquiry. But I had to arrange extra leave, compassionate leave, to get married. Well, my commanding officer in this particular unit was not authorized to give me more than a week's leave, and I'd planned the honeymoon which because of the difficulty of foreign travel at that time, was to take place in the south of Ireland. We'd booked into Ashford Castle over Christmas. And he said, 'I can only grant you seven days' leave, Paddy, but if you take that, and then send me a telegram at the end of that leave requesting an extension, I can grant you an extension.' So that was what happened. And it was a marvellous day in spite of the austerity; it was a magnificent wedding. My bride was extraordinarily late, more than half an hour late arriving at the church, and I began to think I'd been jilted at the altar. However it ensured a good attendance because it ran into the lunchtime

Mr and Mrs Charles Murray.

service at St Anne's Cathedral, and the regular congregation joined in. The reception wedding breakfast was held in what was then the Queen's Hotel – which has since disappeared altogether – in Victoria Street near the Albert Clock. (It became the passport office and is now something else.) And we then proceeded by train to Dublin, we'd no petrol to take a car in those days, although my father had a car so I could have used it, but there wasn't petrol for that sort of a journey. We went by train first of all to Dublin, to Dun Laoghaire for a couple of nights and then on to Cong by train, and that was in those days a very long journey.

*William Wright, born 1921*

## Courting and Marriage

In the St John's I had known Ian Gordon, a friend – I had known him for years and a whole crowd of us were at the Gala one night and he introduced Wilson and me. We met several times at dance and then eventually we started going out together.

My niece came from America for the wedding and I can remember my mother made the dresses, we didn't get married young, we waited, or I just didn't find him until then. But my niece came from America; my brother didn't want her to come because of the Troubles. But at the last minute my sister-in-law said she was coming anyway so my niece persuaded her father to let her go. So eventually she came and there was pandemonium because she wanted to be a bridesmaid. We had asked her, but she said no. I had two bridesmaids and my mother was sitting up half the night trying to get her dress made because she suddenly decided to come. They arrived and the dress wasn't made so it had to be made in a hurry, and that is the only thing I can remember about it.

*Lina Graham, born 1931*

## Wedding Celebrations

It rained all day, it never stopped. We went – now you never went very far in them days – Bangor and back for a walk, down to Bangor. When I came home that night, they would have a wee thing in the house for me, trying to make things comfortable you know. Went down to Bangor, I didn't drink at all, John took a wee drink and the best man took a wee drink, so we went in and out of ice cream shops, they went into the bars. Between the rain and the ice cream, we were frozen to death, me and Lizzie. We were coming down the street, I'll never forget there was only one street in Bangor then, and on the far side of the street a clothes dealer shouted over: 'Did you marry a wee boy called John Hale this morning?' And I says yes. 'He said to tell me if I seen you, that he's down there in that wee bar, to go down, he's waiting on you.' So we went down, and right enough he was as happy as the flowers in May. The wee barman lit a fire for him, and they were sitting, happy days, so we went in and we got a bit of a heat and things like

Maud Meneely and her sister Marina at Floral Hall, Belfast.

Maud Meneely (right) with her friend, Barbara Creighton.

that, you know. But my bridesmaid she took off her shoes, her feet were sore; and she couldn't get them back on to her again. We had to carry her back on to the train, so I never forgot that wedding day till God calls me. We got home right enough and, God love my aunt, they had a wee thing in the house, and John's family was over and that was the first time I'd met them all. It was just a cup of tea and sandwiches and stuff like that.

We lived in my own house, there was nobody there only my mother and I. It wasn't my own house really – it was a rented house – but I went automatically into there.

*Maggie Hale, born 1920*

# CHAPTER 4

# Religion and politics

Charles Murray with his mother's
cousin, Jenny Aitken, in 1913. He is
wearing a Royal Navy uniform made
on board HMS *Hawke*.

## Troubles of 1920/21

I can remember the Norfolk Regiment who were stationed in Seaforde in the Newtownards Road and that was a Catholic area. There was a hall belonged to the Catholic Church, and they were stationed there. They came out one Sunday night and we were coming out of church, where I was at that time going to St Patrick's parish church, Ballymacarrett, and as the people were coming out of church the Norfolk Regiment swung round and charged down the road, and put everybody against the wall with fixed bayonets. They were threatened at that time, and so they didn't know one from another. And of course there we were pinned up against the wall, my brother and sister and myself and after a time we were released and allowed to go home, but you're not allowed to congregate in groups or companies. I can remember a girl called McGregor being shot down at the corner of St Leonard Street. She was standing at the corner of the street another night when the regiment came out across the road at Bryson Street, fired a volley down the road and she was killed at that road. I knew her brother very well, Peter McGregor, but I can remember her being killed that night.

I can remember the Malcolmson brothers who came over from Shankill, very bad crew they were. They came over in a car that was fitted with machine guns and they came along that road firing in every direction, particularly through the Catholic quarters. They had no respect for anyone at all, but then you got the Catholics doing the same thing afterwards – they came and I remember them going down Bright Street opposite Dee Street on the Newtownards Road and breaking all the windows on the way down as they shot into the homes. As they went down to the Albertbridge Road and back to Short Strand again, they were shooting all the way. It was a very, very bad time. I remember the men going over the bridge at Frazer Street, going to their work in Harland and Wolff's engine works and being targeted as they went up the steps of the bridge by snipers that were in the tower of the Roman Catholic church. They had got into the tower and were firing across from there at the bridge.

I didn't take sides of one or the other, but I could see that people whom I knew who were of the Catholic faith were being persecuted by the Protestants, because of what they suffered. They took it out on the people at work, and there was some dreadful things happened, some dreadful things that are forgotten about I suppose.

*Charles Murray, born 1908*

## Trouble at the Yard

When the Protestants in the yard began to band together and to take action they marched on the various departments and had forewarned any Catholics there to get off the site, and if any remained they were in danger. I can remember them chasing them to the edge of the water and they had to swim for it, those that could swim. That was what they used to call 'deep water wharf' where the ships where fitted out before going to sea, but that was it.

Practically every one of them carried

William Austin at the forensic lab in Belfast following a bomb, 1990s.

arms, because they were threatened as they went home and targeted even in their homes, some of them, depending where they lived. It was a terrible time.

*Charles Murray, born 1908*

## Remembering the Troubles

I can remember one of the very first things that happened was the blowing up of the power lines. there was a couple of big power stations blown up, and I can remember that happened when I was in my last year at school. Because I lived in the country, North Down, the Troubles didn't impact immediately, it was only that when you went into places like East Belfast where I had relations and friends, and you started to realize that it had a bigger impact on them, you know, the working class areas there. Troubles never impacted on me much, there was only once when I was in a warehouse buying something, somebody stuck a gun in my face. It was a hold-up – a robbery – but it was politically motivated, they were out looking for money to buy guns, but you don't feel it affects you much at the time. The chap just wanted me to stand there while he pulled money out of the till. Things like that, I suppose you feel it's unreal: I can remember I just walked back slowly and actually walked backwards until I got behind a big carousel of some sort, then ran off down to the bottom of the warehouse, where there were two or three people talking, didn't know what was going on at the other end. And I was trying to find a phone, to phone the police, and couldn't really get anybody to pay any attention to what I was saying. But I suppose that in a way was my closest brush with the Troubles other than everybody else saying things, being caught up in bomb scares and so on, but I imagine maybe that happened to everybody in Northern Ireland.

*Ruth McAllister, born 1951*

## Beliefs and Fears

I wasn't dogmatic about it, I just let my daughter come to her own decision. I tried to teach her the right thing and she went to Sunday school and she went to Bible class, and that kind of thing. Then whenever she was sixteen there was a mission in Duncairn church and she waited behind and she became a Christian and she still is a Christian, in England. She goes to the United Reform Church in England and she's an elder in the Church there. But her children aren't religious minded at all, they don't bother.

But I feel that prayer is a very important thing in life and God has been very good to me. Although I was widowed in '71 when I was only fifty-three – but I felt that God had a reason for that. I don't really know why he took my lovely husband away but I will know one day why.

*Margaret Mills, born 1918*

## Sundays

We weren't allowed to do anything on Sunday. I mean if you didn't clean your shoes on Saturday for going

Belmont Primary School, where Ruby Purdy was educated.

to church on Sunday you had to go with them dirty. We had a wireless but that only went on on Sunday for the news or for a church service, so we were brought up quite strictly like that.

*Maud Meneely, born 1929*

## 'Never Borrow Anything'

I feel that you have to have a faith, you know to continue with life, after all what is life worth, if there's not going to be something, at the end of it? And we were always taught as children, there wasn't any really evangelical type of talk in the home. But we were always taught to be truthful and to never deny anything, if you'd done anything wrong, you were always taught to own up to it, and not to tell any lies to anybody. And I think it stuck with me, and it was the same even when I was married and had the family, and that was one thing that my husband was very strict on, he always used to say 'never borrow anything'.

*Ruby Purdy, born 1914*

## Faith in the Afterlife

I think that it's the only meaning there is in life really. I mean, I can't see anything else that explains how life on earth came about, I can't really subscribe to this Big Bang thing. I think there must be more than that to regulate life the way it is, so yes I think it is very important to me, particularly through bad times. And I've had some: my only brother was killed in a farm

accident when he was just married for a couple of years, and that was very difficult. Now he was drowned in one of those slurry tanks that they have in the country. Nobody's ever sure what happened. He had a man working at it clearing it out, and it's thought that this man had gone down into it to retrieve something that had fallen in, and that my brother went in after him to try to save him and he was drowned in that, when he had two small children, the first of them only months old. That was very difficult for me, and I think you can either lose your faith at a time like that or you can be strengthened by it.

Then again my brother's only son he was killed in a road accident when he was only nineteen so that was a difficult time for our family as well.

I don't have much concept of what it's like but I believe strongly that there is something. I don't believe that we're gone and that's it. But I think it's difficult to imagine what it's going to be like, I think that it's just a thing we don't understand, and we have to take it for granted.

*Maud Meneely, born 1929*

## Socialism and Religion

When I was a young guy I had friends – some of them were university students, some weren't – but they tended to be sceptics and very left wing, and I would have gone along with all that. But you see one has to remember in those days that there was a lot of that coming from the major universities. Socialism was very important to a lot of people, a huge

# Strandtown

There was Legge's at the corner where we used to buy our shoes,
The next shop down was Mr Smyth's where we bought our penny chews.
Across the road was Campbell's, the clothes shop, it was there,
And three doors down was Stirling's, the man who cut your hair.

One up from him was Billy Neill's, whose fruits you could not lick,
And you couldn't get a word in 'cause he talked that bloomin' quick.
Facing him was Dawson's, the little hardware shop,
Two doors up was Fowler's where you got a lollipop.

On the same block was McCracken's – its food there was no nicer,
And across the way was Milligan's where you watched the bacon slicer.
Now you all remember Christie's, he's the man that sold the fish,
Who put the whitewash on his windows to sell his tasty dish.

There was Mortimer's, the Belmont, two wee sweetie shops,
And you mind the butcher's, Hanna's, where they sold delicious chops.
Mr Simpson owned the chipper you call the 'Silver Leaf'
And we all remember Morrow, the man that hurt your teeth.

There was Nelson's Off Sales on the road, he used to make us merry,
And Cissie's in Dundela Street – you mind the woman with the beret?
There was Henry's at the entry where you bought a walnut whip,
And the parlour house on the Belmont Road where the woman fixed your zip.

There was Buckley's on the corner where you went to buy your tools,
And Roberts' up the road a bit that kitted out for schools.
Then Mr Smyth the bootmender, he used to fix your shoes,
And remember Gerry Patterson's whose papers told the news.

There was Morrison's the chemist, who used to keep us well,
And Jennings' home bakery where you couldn't beat the smell.
There was Edwards' the shoe shop where we bought our summer sandals,
And Kate's wee shop in Wilgar Street, where you went to hear the scandals.

There was Batman on the pictures – as kids we were mad keen –
It was on the Strand and it only had one screen.
That was Strandtown in the sixties – you knew it couldn't last.
Let's all look to the future, but don't forget the past.

Hammy McClements

A poem about Strandtown in the sixties, where Ruby Purdy grew up.

David and Ruby Purdy play host to three Labour Party members visiting Belfast in the early 1960s. From left to right: Ruby Purdy, Lord Robins, Jim Callaghan, Winnie Bleakley and Arthur Bottomley.

number of intellectuals were socialists, so it was a thing that was widespread. I gradually came away from the socialism because I could see that in practice it wasn't working. I don't want to offend anyone, but going hard at socialism is a mistake because you could see what had happened in Eastern Europe and in the new socialist countries of Poland and Czechoslovakia and Hungary and so on, it just simply wasn't working and it was a frightful mess. I gradually got to thinking about these things: the life force, the things that you could see if you looked at it through a microscope, a living cell, and saw all that activity, and if you looked into the night sky and saw the immensity of space and the organization of the solar system and so on. There had to be something in my view something that produced that, some intelligence. So I just gradually, and I mean gradually, came to accept that there was more to life.

*William Austin, born 1926*

## Husband's Politics

Oh yes, he was always involved in politics, I think that's what brought him to York Street as well. When he started going to York Street, he was in the old city Labour Party, at the same time that my brother joined. I can't remember where they met, probably in York Street, in the old labour hall, I'm not sure but there was a few of the people in the church belonging to it too. And David was always inclined to be with the Labour Party. After the war we came back to Hillsborough, then from Hillsborough, we got a house on the Holywood Road, and at that time there was a labour hall down in Townsley Street. At that time, the Daily Herald was the Labour paper, and my husband used to go into this shop on the Holywood road to get the paper, and that was where he met David Bleakley and they were both buying the Daily Herald. That was how they got talking. Well then, David Bleakley came to the door one evening, David had said where he lived you see, so David Bleakley came to the door and I opened the door and he stood and looked at me, couldn't believe that it was me, cause he knew me from when we grew up together. But he didn't know that I was married to David Purdy, so when he saw me at the door he was all pleased, when he saw who it was, so from that on we got very friendly. David Bleakley wasn't married of course at that time; he was going with Winnie Wason, but they used to come and stay in my house, and when we were going some place, Winnie and David would have stayed in and looked after the children while we went out, babysitting as they call it now. And the strange thing was when David got married and they had their children, my eldest boy used to go up and babysit for them.

Well, I think it reinforced them really. We were always Labour inclined

David Purdy, David Bleakley, Peter Bleakley, Winnie Bleakley and Ruby Purdy in 1958, while campaigning for the Northern Ireland Labour Party in the Victoria constituency in Belfast.

but we seemed to get more involved and then we had the hall in Townsley Street, which was a rented hall. It was actually above a blacksmith's forge, in fact in that blacksmith's forge, many a time my father used to get work done in it. He knew the blacksmith, anyway; the blacksmith's son and my brothers were at school together. But anyhow, we had the hall in Townsley Street, and my husband always wanted to get a proper hall of our own, and we talked about it for years, in fact he used to run whist drives in the hall, and he always said that money was for the building fund. And always if there was any money at all came in on anything, it went into the building fund, and although David never lived to see it, when the building fund was finished, there was quite a bit of money in it. After David Purdy died David Bleakley actually lost his seat. Right in the middle of the election David died, he died on the Saturday night and the election was the following Thursday and then David lost his seat that time to Roy Bradford. Shortly after that, he went to lecture in a Methodist college, and he wasn't very long in Methody when he got a secondment to Givacona in Africa, in Tanzania, and he went out. He took his family, Winnie and the three boys, and went out to Tanzania, and was teaching in Givacona. He was there for about, I think, about a year and a half, or two years maybe. But by that time I had moved to Orby Drive to stay with a nephew for about a year, and then they built Kilbroney House on the Cregagh Road, and I got a flat in it, and Michael and I came to live in it. And then David Bleakley of course kept in correspondence with us, and he wrote to

say that he wanted to get the boys, the two older boys back, it was time they were old enough to go to the grammar school, and he wanted to get them back before he would come home. So he wrote to see if they could come and stay with Michael and I. So I only had the two bedrooms in the flat but I went and bought a pair of bunk beds, and put them into Michael's room, and the three boys slept in the one room. And sometimes it was like bedlam at night. I used to have to rap the wall when the three of them got into the one room. But they came and they stayed with me, I think they came about the beginning of January, and they were there till David, when he came home, I think about the month of May or June. They were with me four or five months, anyhow, and we had quite a happy time. Many a time there was rows with the boys, but isn't that always the way? They were like one family, there was nothing really bad about it, just the usual play with boys.

*Ruby Purdy, born 1914*

## Father's Politics

Well I always felt that you know, we were always against the old fashioned Ulster Unionist Party. We thought that you know, that the Labour Party was more for the common people, and that was really what was interesting, what really got us interested in going to the ILP.

*Ruby Purdy, born 1914*

A Group of York Street church members on a visit to Ballee church in 1938.

## Beliefs

If you really start to think of it, the Ten Commandments, if you follow them, they really are the rules for living. I think that I've really, while not being religious, I've tried to follow the Ten Commandments, and the respect and the trust which they imply. I try the best I can to treat everybody in the best way possible and hope that in actual fact satisfies them, and hope that it satisfies me. I think that's the concept of religion, and I think that maybe goes back to an experience which I had with people way back, of humanists and free thinkers and people like that, and hearing their ideas and how they feel.

*Clive Hughes, born 1939*

## Church and Politics

Well, when the Reverend A.L. Agnew came as a young minister in 1923 to York Street, it had been lying more or less derelict. They hadn't had a minister for quite some time, and he was just ordained and came to take over York Street, in 1923. My eldest brother was very much interested in different churches at that time, and the evangelist Nicholson came to Belfast, I think he originally was from Northern Ireland, but he been in America and he had come to Belfast and he talked about Doctor Agnew. He wasn't Doctor Agnew then, he was only the Reverend A.L. but the Reverend A.L. challenged Nicholson to a debate, which he didn't turn up to. But he had advertised a

97

service, 'Christ or Nicholson', in the York Street, and my brother went to hear it, and he came home so enthusiastic about this young minister, that he got my mother and father to go. I was only about ten year old at the time, and of course I went with them, to York Street. And from that on we didn't go back to St Mark's. We started going to York Street Sunday evenings; my mother and father didn't always go in the morning, they always went in the evening. But we started going in the morning to church, and then as well as that they started a fellowship, in the afternoon. We had various speakers, oh many varieties of speakers: we had Mormons used to come to it, and we had a lot of political figures, and different religious figures of all denominations came and talked on Sunday afternoons. We had a debate, and then as well as that, Tommy Carnduff, who was the shipyard poet, he was a member of the Church, and any of the plays that he wrote, they were talked over in the Guild on a Sunday, in the fellowship on a Sunday afternoon. They talked, they actually read his plays there before they went into any of the theatres. Nearly every night was taken up in York Street because they had a men's club on a Monday night, and on Tuesday night they went to the swimming club, in the Falls baths. Wednesday was choir practice, I joined the choir then, and Thursday there was a dramatic society. And Doc Agnew was very much involved in all of these things, because he was a great swimmer. He didn't involve himself in the choir but in the dramatic society, he was involved in it. And on Friday nights they had what they called the games club, and they just had all sorts of games, not very much organized, more or less table tennis, and things like that. And then on Saturday was the guild which was like a dance, and we had a band used to come, it was actually like a one man band, just drums and a girl on the piano. And we very often had people coming even to talk at it as well. Sunday afternoon was the main day for the fellowship and it's all classes of people we had then, very interesting too. It meant that our whole life nearly was taken up, you didn't go to everything but you went to most of them. And then there was the ILP hall which was the Independent Labour Party, they had their hall across the street, in York Street. And my brother, my eldest brother and my father got more or less involved in the ILP, and I very often went if there was public meetings, I very often went with them as a child to those meetings.

*Ruby Purdy, born 1914*

## A.L. Agnew

Well he was a man that had a great bit of thought for people – what we would call underdogs – he was. He wasn't only involved in preaching the gospel, but he did a lot of good works amongst the poor people, and he was a very thoughtful person. And he got involved with all sorts of things. He married then Dr Isabel Caldwell, her father was a doctor in York Street. And they met and were married about 1932, I think it was. He was always involved in helping people, or people used to come in round the church, and nobody

The Revd Dr A.L. Agnew, minister at York Street Non-Subscribing Presbyterian church in Belfast.

ever went away empty-handed, and at night after the evening service, we always made tea. I think we were about the first church in Belfast who started making tea after the service, and the women of the church did it in turns, they had a rota, and a couple of women would do it one night, and a couple more the next night, and it was always visitors first. Doctor he always used to say, 'FHB', family hold back until the visitors had their tea, and then of course everybody else had a cup of tea, and whatever was made afterwards.

He was a real socialist, because he practised what he preached as well, and I think that was what made us go so much to it, and got involved in it. Well then of course, York Street, when the war started then, York Street was blitzed in 1941. And there was a church of All Souls, in Elmwood Avenue, and they had a very small congregation and no minister but a very good building, and when York Street was, it was completely demolished in the Blitz. And Doctor knew then, the presbytery arranged that York Street could move their congregation up to All Souls, Elmwood Avenue. So that's where we moved in 1941. I was married and had two of a family at that time and we were blitzed and we had to move out. The house was, well, not destroyed but it was badly damaged, and we moved out. By that time my brother had a chemist shop in Hillsborough, and there was a farmer, a customer of his, who had a house, an empty house, about a mile and a half out of Hillsborough, and we were able to rent it, and go down there. It was bedlam in the house, because there were nineteen of us in the one house, and there were eight children and three of

those children were under a year old, so you may guess what it was like then.

*Ruby Purdy, born 1914*

## St Mark's Services

In those days in St Mark's church, I suppose in all the churches, people at that time rented a pew, and you paid so much a year, and those mostly who paid a big amount of money were at the front of the church. Well we weren't at the front of the church, we were well further down nearer the back of the church, but everybody sat in their own seats in those days. I don't think it's the same now, but you rented a pew and that was your pew, while the services were there. But, when I was very small, we didn't go to church as often, we went to Sunday school, which was held in the old school, what used to be Strandtown National School, at Gelsons' corner. It actually was originally the St Mark's church before the church was built on the Holywood Road. There was a bell actually on the building of Strandtown School, and it was rather churchy-like in the building. But as I say when I was very small, we didn't go on to church, my father used to come and meet us coming out of Sunday school, and he would take the older ones, my sister and my two older brothers, he took them on to church. Tommy, the one next to me, we would go on home, as it was coming up dinner time by that time. But then when we went home and had our lunch we'd be back then to Sunday school in the afternoon. Then my father used to meet us in the summertime and take us away out for a walk up round the Castlereagh Hills.

*Ruby Purdy, born 1914*

## Friends in the Church

I feel without a faith I don't know how I would have managed. I had breast cancer some years ago, and that was in 1991, and really and truly my friends in church – I belong to the Mothers' Union in the Church of Ireland – and they were absolutely wonderful, and upheld me, you know, with prayers. And I feel that my faith has sustained me through so many things in life – I mean losing my husband, when the children were little, and all that – it's been wonderful, I couldn't live without it.

*Sheila Hughes, born 1928*

## Varied Religions

I am trying to think what age I would have been – I suppose about fourteen, fifteen. I don't know exactly know how, but through a friend I was brought to a meeting of the Crusaders' Union. Now, I don't know whether you've ever heard of the Crusaders' Union but they were a sort of union, it sounds very snobbish of secondary schoolboys, who attended Bible classes in the afternoon. And together with my friends we were very regular attenders at this thing. They appealed to boys because they had a lot of activities and they held an annual camp at Castlerock, which we all went to and had great fun. A little bit overloaded on the religious side in that

our camp started with a prayer meeting in the morning and a prayer meeting in the afternoon, and a prayer meeting in the evening. And we all sang rousing choruses of an evangelical nature, camped around in County Londonderry, singing our songs at the top of our voices and it was good fun. And I became so involved that in fact when the Belfast branch of the Crusaders' Union lost their premises for meeting which had been the Presbyterian hostel, my father suggested them meeting in our homes, just a small group, and that happened. I broke with that when I went to London. I was away from it; I was not, had never been a tremendously regular church attender, but we did go to churches. As a family my parents were not fervent church attenders; they were members of a church and supported their church, attended church from time to time, but not on a regular basis. My father having lived abroad for a number of years had got away from the general Northern Ireland attitude on religion, but we were brought up in a Christian home. Anyway I lost touch with the Crusaders' Union on going to London, although in fact I could have transferred as there were branches of the Crusaders in parts of London, but I chose not to do so. And then as I went in to the air force, it began to distance itself from me, or me from it, a bit more. For a start these desert stations where I was, we didn't support anything like a padre on a regular basis anyway, from time to time a padre would arrive at the camp. It didn't really very much matter whether he was Church of Ireland, Roman Catholic or other denominations, or for that matter Jewish Rabbis. One usually attended their service out of respect for the man. But I was learning an awful lot about other religions, the Jewish faith, which appealed to me a lot. With Muslim faith I found a great deal to commend it, and later when I went to India I learnt a little bit about Buddhism, not particularly much about Hinduism, it seemed a little bit weird to me. But I think one of the things that influenced a lot was the fact that I found that those of our number who were keenly religious people were those who were most frightened of death, and this to me seemed something of an anomaly. If the life to come was all so marvellous why did they not want to go there? It seemed strange to me. Gradually over the years, the deep-set faith dwindled, and I became certainly not an atheist but an agnostic I would say. I don't know – its possible I don't know, I don't see how man can know, one can believe but one can't know.

The stories were only coming through in the latter part of the war of the brutality of the Nazis against the Jewish people. And I couldn't see how a country calling itself Christian could behave in this way. When I say I ceased to believe, I am certain that such a person as Jesus Christ existed – a splendid person, a great teacher, set a code of moral behaviour and values, which everyone should follow whatever their faith. But not necessarily the Son of God. If you speak to the average ex-serviceman, he is by no means a warmongerer. In fact most ex-servicemen are strong pacifists, but nevertheless they don't want the past forgotten.

*William Wright, born 1921*

# CHAPTER 5

# *Wartime*

A letter confirming Charles Murray's appointment as an ARP instructor, 1941.

## Incendiary Bomb

One of the incendiary bombs had dropped in our street and I saw it dropping and I panicked and started to shout, but not my sister. This timid sister of mine, she lifted a sandbag and went and threw it over on the incendiary bomb, so it just shows you.

*Margaret Mills, born 1918*

## The War Years

The war years affected us very little, because we never were short of food, because on the farm we grew our own food. Listening to the war on the radio, I mean Belfast sounded as far away to us probably as America does nowadays, we'd never been there. I had a sister who was working at the time at Ballyclare and the only concern we had was really concern for her, knowing that that was quite close to Belfast, but it didn't really affect us at all. For meat, we had chickens, etc. We even would have killed a pig and salted it up for bacon so we didn't want for anything at all during the war.

There were quite a number of evacuees. We didn't have any because we had a small house and a big family, but some of the farmers beside us had evacuees and we got to know them quite well.

*Maud Meneely, born 1929*

## Feelings Towards the Germans

I didn't know them as well as I know them now, but I thought there was a meanness about them, and a feeling to grab everything they could get their hands on. You know, you wouldn't have touched anything German with a forty-foot pole, in those days.

*Lena Purdy, born 1901*

## The Blitz

I remember 1941 very well in fact, especially living where I did right down in the city centre, and there were a lot of casualties in and around there. They were a tight community just across Clifton Street, there was a church there, I think it was the Holy Trinity church, and it was destroyed. There were many people lost their lives in that area, it was so close to the city centre, so close, you might say, down to the docks. Well, if they missed their target at the docks or the city centre, they hit the surrounding areas and a lot of people lived very close to the city centre in those days in Belfast.

There was great confusion and no-one knew what to do. The air-raid shelters were so inadequate really, I mean they were little brick boxes with concrete roofs on them, and other ones were long with concrete blocks. In many instances the walls of the air raid shelters where blown in and then of course the concrete roof just fell down on top of people; there were a lot of casualties in that way. But they were very good in the sense that there were a lot of fire bombs rained down on

Belfast. There was a lot of damage in Belfast related to firebombs – incendiaries as we called them – and possibly those air-raid shelters were grand in that sense, because if you got an incendiary through the roof of a house, well there was really great danger in that. Certainly, as I'm saying, the air-raid shelters I felt were grand as a guard against incendiaries, but certainly not against high explosives.

*Paddy McAteer, born 1928*

## Easter Tuesday Blitz

I always remember the night that my Aunt May, my mother's sister, was blitzed out, it was terrible. There was a shelter outside the door in Craigavad Street, they had built wee brick shelters, you see, right up, and we were in the one outside, it was nearly outside our door. I remember the planes going up over us, and they were saying, 'Oh, that's Duncairn Gardens district's getting that', it kept going up over it. Now that was the Easter Tuesday Blitz, and my Aunt May had had all children in that day for Easter, the ones round the door, for she only had the one son. Our Ronnie was only three and all his wee chums were killed in that street, it was terrible. Hogarth Street got it very, very bad. Well then, my Aunt May, she went down to Whiteabbey, so then we got it on 5 May and I was down in Whiteabbey with my aunt. I came to the station and people were saying, 'Oh, it's terrible round facing the railway'. That's where we lived, and they mentioned the big shelter at the corner of Rowan Street, so I knew that was us.

I came up on the train, and that was the time people out of the church had taken my mother and father down to Islandmagee, and the place was wrecked. It was really wrecked all round but there was no deaths, because people had got a lesson from the Hogarth Street one, you see. But now they used to have good fun in the shelters like, you could have laughed at it now. We had one character and he would have got us all singing 'Come Back Paddy Reilly to Ballyjamesduff' and all this. I remember that night of the Hogarth Street one, my father came out of the shelter, and we had an old man lived next door to us on his own, and whatever had happened, he had a window broken. But we had no windows or anything broken, but it must have been the blast had knocked his window in. He said, 'Oh, look at my windows!' and he says, 'Youse haven't got a window smashed.' My father says 'No, I sent Hitler up our address, you know.' You could have made fun of it at the time, although it was serious.

*Nessie McNamee, born 1921*

## Evacuees from Belfast

I was teaching at school you see, and all of a sudden one day I had fourteen children and the next day I had forty-eight. They walked out of Belfast, the people. When I say they walked, they must have camped, you know, along the road or something like that, it was summertime anyway. They walked out into Crossgar and just took over. And it was no joke: that was my classroom, I don't know how many would have been

# EMPIRE THEATRE
## BELFAST.

---
❈
---

## 100th EDITION OF
### THE RECORD-BREAKING REVUE
# "COME TO THE SHOW"

---
❈
---

# · Souvenir ·

### OF THE

# Gala Performance

### ON

# Thursday, 8th July, 1943.

ENTIRE PROCEEDS TO—
THE GOVERNOR'S FUND FOR THE RED CROSS AND ALL WAR CHARITIES.

---
❈
---

UNDER THE DISTINGUISHED PATRONAGE OF
Their Graces The Duke and Duchess of Abercorn.

The Right Hon. The Prime Minister (Sir Basil Brooke, Bart.)
and Lady Brooke.

The Right Hon. The Lord Mayor (Sir Crawford M'Cullagh, Bart.)

---
❈
---

Relayed by the B.B.C., 7—7.30 p.m.
FORCES PROGRAMME.

A souvenir programme from the Empire Theatre, Belfast, 1943.

in the other rooms, you see. Well then these people had to get billets, and then the head teacher had to go round finding billets for these people. I can tell you a story about that. I went to one lady and we were always very polite to say, 'And how many children have you and what accommodation have you?' So we said this to this lady, and she says she had seventeen children. I got the hold of the two teachers, 'Come on', I said, 'we can't do anything here.' Well, she said, 'I could let you sleep in the barn, somebody could sleep in the barn', she said. But seventeen children – there must have been a lot of them gone, you know they weren't all there.

*Lena Purdy, born 1901*

## The Empire Theatre

What happened was, whenever the bombing raid came, of course then the theatre emptied as you can imagine, but they prided themselves in that they never closed. And I had a friend Billy Barry, she was the sister of Norma Barry, and she was in the troupe. She was the head girl in the troupe, and I saw her just recently, she lives in Dublin, she has a big theatre school still there in Dublin. And she was telling me, I remember so well, whenever the Blitz came, she said that there were only three people the night after that, you know. But we kept going and then it built up and built up and built up, you know. So that again, as I said, every night then we had packed houses.

*Sheila Hughes, born 1928*

## Arrival in London

This love of aircraft remained with me subsequently when I went to live in London, in February of 1939. I took every opportunity to visit RAF stations and air displays. Well the drums of war were sounding faintly at that time; there had been a great recruitment drive for the various ancillary services, the Royal Naval Reserve, the Territorial Army and of course the Royal Air Force Reserve, and together with two colleagues in my office we applied to join the RAFVR. This wasn't entirely an unselfish move on our behalf, because one of the things about it was that you got paid for attendance and at the RAFVR, you got extra leave from the civil service, an extra fortnight a year, to go to camp. And if you did those things you got a bounty of £12 a year, and that was an important bit when you were only earning £75 a year – a £12 bounty seems attractive. However before our applications could be processed, the war broke out, and the idea of the recruitment of the RAFVR was shelved. However my two colleagues and myself still had this feeling that we would like to get in, and learn to fly. We discovered however that recruitment had temporarily closed on the outbreak of war, until all these reserve forces could be mobilized. It was not until October of that year, 1939, that recruitment opened. Well now we didn't know much about the Royal Air Force and when we applied at the recruiting station we were told that there were no vacancies for any air crew whatsoever, not to join as pilot, or observer or air gunner. This was rather disappointing, but nevertheless we

Elementary trainer *Fleet Finch*, Ontario, Canada, in July 1941.

signed up to be ordinary aircraft hands, on general duties.

*William Wright, born 1921*

## Declaration of War

I was in my digs. The previous day, Saturday 2 September, on my way to the office I had seen as I passed the various schools on route to my office, these lines and lines of school children, each with their little cardboard box with its gas mask and a little cardboard suitcase and a label attached to them as they were evacuated from the city. So we were pretty certain that the inevitable was coming, and that particular Sunday I woke and I had a small radio set, a rented radio set in my room, and I switched it on just after I woke to catch an announcement. It said plainly, stand by for an important announcement, so naturally enough I was glued to the set, and this message was repeated and repeated and repeated. And after a few minutes they made an announcement to the effect that the Prime Minister would speak to the nation at 11 o'clock. Well of course I was up and dressed and shaved, and down for breakfast, and I understand the weather that day in Northern Ireland was absolutely foul, but in London it was a beautiful day, it was a lovely September morning, with sunshine. We, the guests of this establishment, had volunteered to assist our landlady in converting a basement area into a sort of refuge room or a shelter. So the young men were all busily engaged in the garden with spades, filling sandbags, and the few girls in the digs would sew

William Wright newly commissioned as Pilot Officer, 1941.

William Wright outside the officers' mess tent at Bu Amud in 1943, with 'Pooch'.

these up and we would put them in place round the windows and doors. And as 11 o'clock approached one of the residents brought his large radio baffle board to the back window and turned on the radio. We stopped work and we heard Chamberlain make his very famous announcement and as he finished with the words '...and I have to tell you now that a state of war exists between us and Germany', and he'd hardly finished speaking and we had hardly time to react, before the sirens sounded. Well we'd been brought up with a picture mostly from the Spanish Civil War of cities being bombed and we thought well this is it, this is how the Germans are going to open the war with a massive attack on London, and we took things very seriously. We all had left our gas masks in our bedrooms and there was a mass exodus and race up the stairs to get the gas masks. I can still remember the chap whom I shared with had obviously preceded me and when I entered the room all I could see where his feet projecting from under the bed where he decided it would be a safer place. However that air-raid warning turned out to be a false alarm. I gather it was a French plane that had been sighted over the Channel and mistakenly identified as enemy. So it was only a matter of minutes before the all-clear sounded and everything calmed down again. But there was an air of excitement and we all went out on the streets to see the special constables wearing steel helmets, parading the streets. The blackout we were not to experience properly until that night, but there had been one week previously a rehearsal of a blackout of Lambeth. And this was treated actually with great hilarity and it was all great fun. A crowd of us went by bus into the West End and wandered round the streets with little dimmed out pocket torches and thought it was rollicking fun. But this was the real thing.

*William Wright, born 1921*

## Getting My Wings

In December in '41 came the big day when those of us who had completed the course qualified and were granted our wings, and they made quite a ceremony of that in Canada, laid on a sort of open day. Canadians amongst us were allowed to have their families there to see them be presented with their wings, and we of course did not have families in Canada, but we'd made quite a few friends. I know I had two delightful young ladies, sisters who travelled all the way from St Katherine's, to see me get my wings. This was a family who had befriended us, their parents took us into their home when we had any free time, and this was quite exciting. At that time we all assumed that we would be sergeant pilot when we qualified; however, unknown to us, one third of the course were to be granted commissions, and it was not until I had my wings painted on, pinned on my tunic and was signing for my leave pass travel warrant, that I was addressed for the first time as Pilot Officer and was told I had been an officer with effect from one minute past midnight that day.

*William Wright, born 1921*

## Phantom Voice

I had only time for a short burst of machine gun fire, when I heard a loud bang and I realized my own aircraft had been hit. At that time I thought it was only the aeroplane but as I found out later I had been wounded in the leg and in the chest and in the hand. I didn't really discover that until I saw blood on the instrument panel, because there was no pain at that time. But I'd time to go home and initially try to look for a place in case I had to force-land. However the aircraft kept flying alright, and I made my way from the south of the island, heading back to Africa again.

I had a rather strange experience. I had been losing rather a lot of blood and was a wee bit worried about passing out in the cockpit which would have meant going into the sea and sudden death. And I had contemplated baling out over the sea but I realized that, not only would my parachute be likely to be shot at in the attack, but also my 'Mae West' – my life jacket – would be punctured. So I stayed on at what I was doing, and eventually saw the coast of north Africa coming up. I realized that I would not have flown a true course back; I had merely set my compass on 180 due south, and flown knowing I couldn't miss Africa. But on arrival at the shore I realized that I had been blown somewhat off my dead reckoning course and I didn't recognize just where I was. Now what fuel I had was running out and I had to make a decision fairly quickly: was I going to turn left – travel east – or was I going to turn right and travel west, until I came to the airfield? And I called up on my radio and asked for a homing which was not an uncommon thing, just request emergency homing, and ground control would take a fix and give you a course to steer. However I got no reply which was unusual, I called again and no reply, and again, still no reply. And then in my earphones I heard a voice that I knew, the voice of Sergeant Dave Horsley who was with us on the raid, and he said, 'Paddy, this is Dave, steer 270', so that was all the information I needed, put myself on a westerly heading and in a few short minutes I saw a familiar piece of coastline that I knew, the airfield ahead. And although there was a sandstorm blowing I was able to land, and I was lifted out of the cockpit and rushed to the doctor's surgery in a tent, who had a look at my wounds, gave me a shot of morphine and dressed the wounds lightly. I was put in an ambulance and taken to a casualty clearing centre, which was like a mini-hospital, again a tented hospital, where the nurses took charge. And after I'd been made comfortable some of the other pilots from the squadron came to visit me, including the commanding officer, and they were pleased to see that I was as well as I was. I said, 'Where is Dave Horsley? I want to thank him for putting me on a course.' And everybody went a bit quiet, and the CO said, 'Dave's not with us', and I said, 'Well, he told me to steer a westerly course.' They said, 'You must be mistaken, Paddy. Dave is dead; he went into the sea just after we left the coast of Crete.' I've never explained what this was, but I am quite sure in my own mind that I heard his voice. But that was by the way.

*William Wright, born 1921*

William Wright at the tail of a Hurricane IIC in Burma, 1944.

## The End of the War

I had been posted back from Burma. I had done two tours of operations and they decided to give me a rest, so I was sent back to the Middle East again, and sent again to training command, where I was made chief flying instructor at an operational training unit on the Suez Canal, which was very routine flying. The war in Europe was coming to an end, it was quite obvious that that was going to happen. The one in Europe had very little to do with us, we were training pilots to fight the Japanese in the Far East, and the feeling at that time was that war would go on for at least another three years, possibly more. So when the expected announcement of VE Day – Victory in Europe – came about, it was a bit of an anticlimax. We were all obviously very pleased but it had very little to do with us, and our training programme continued as before. The big surprise, however, came later in August. None of us had any pre-knowledge of anything about atom bombs at all, in fact we knew very little about jet aircraft. We'd heard rumours that there were jets, but we knew nothing about them. And I remember well going into breakfast, and the commanding officer, the group captain was there already. He said, 'Paddy, have you heard the news? They've dropped a bomb the size of a cricket ball in Japan', and he says it's got the effect of thousands of tons of high explosives. And we quite frankly didn't believe this story – it sounded like a rumour – and then we had the confirmation. Then the second bomb was dropped and we couldn't see how the Japanese could carry on against such a weapon. And then quite suddenly came the announcement that the Japanese had surrendered. Now that was an exciting time, the whole station went mad, all flying was cancelled, long-hidden stocks of booze were broken out, and it became one long party. The officers went down to the airmen's mess and sang to them, and played musical instruments. And that night we had a barbecue in the middle of the airfield, did a spit roasting of a camel, a young camel. It wasn't very good eating but it was fun roasting it. The whole thing was full of joy. And then the following day of course we did carry on with training but on a much lighter programme, because we weren't really sure what we were training people to do. In fact many of the pilots who were going through at that time, finished up never seeing a squadron and many of them shifted to the transport section for driving trucks and doing other air force jobs.

*William Wright, born 1921*

# CHAPTER 6
## Changes and the future

William Hutton in a Belfast street, 1951.

## Attitudes to Authority

When a minister of religion would come into your home you stood up in my younger days, as a mark of respect, and what he said was relied upon as being the truth. You looked upon him as a man of God, a representative. That doesn't happen today; today, if the minister would appear in his gown they would call him a crow, they would make jest of him as though he was trying to put on a show. I fear that there isn't the same interest or respect shown. Chivalry today is an unheard-of word, it's dropped out of the vocabulary altogether. When an elderly person gets onto a bus today he stands if the bus if full. In my younger days a young person would have got up and given you the seat, or would have assisted you on the tram. But not today: there's a clambering, 'me first', and you get this when they're coming out of school. They haven't time to wait, they're running wild to get into the bus queue and as soon as they open the door everybody rushes to the door. And so very elderly people can be knocked over and injured under these circumstances. There is no respect, that's gone.

*Charles Murray, born 1908*

## Young People

I do feel that young people are being led to appreciate things on the television which to me are coarse and I suppose I am saying television because I think the vision – looking at the thing – is different from just hearing it. And I feel that they're learning to appreciate things which are really to me are rude and crude. There are people with such ill manners and so on, getting that across as being the way to live, this is how you enjoy yourself. And I'd say, my two grandchildren, I have no fault to find with them at all, I have a great chat with them, and they are well mannered and so on. Newspapers that you read and even books that you're recommended to read, sometimes they're really not. Crude, rough: a lot of sort of niceties have gone out of life to me, but again in my own circle and in the things that I go to, there are a lot of very nice people and I enjoy going to those.

*Peg Armstrong, born 1919*

## Children Today

I think there's too many pressures on children nowadays. There's too many pressures in school to do well; we weren't pressurised like that, we lived a more carefree life. We played a lot and there was a tennis tournament, where the boat club is, there used to be a tennis tournament up there, and we always looked forward to every June at the tennis tournament. There used to be lovely cars came up to bring the players and we used to go along and admire all the cars, but we wouldn't have touched them, we never touched the cars.

Even at the corner of the street where I lived there was a lamp post and we used to put a rope up on the lamp post and swing round the lamp, and if we saw a policeman coming we would have run into the house, we wouldn't have faced him, we would have just run away. Nowadays I think they stand up to policemen and policemen have a bad

Margaret Mills with her husband and daughter in Belfast city centre, 1950.

Margaret Mills with her mother and daughter, Belfast, 1949.

time with some of the children
nowadays – they're not afraid. Well,
maybe it's a good idea that they're not
afraid of them any more, but we were
afraid of them.

*Margaret Mills, born 1918*

## Graciousness that has Gone

Men looked after women, and
everyone looked after children
and there was a politeness and you
didn't use bad language. Well, you
might have used it but only on certain
occasions and you certainly wouldn't
have done it in public. There was a
feeling that you had to be respectable,
this was driven into you: be nice to

people, be friendly to people, open
doors for people, and get up for people
and it was very pleasant in that sense, it
was a genteel existence.

I get the feeling nowadays, watching
people and listening to people, that
they've got too many worries about the
mortgage, living up to a lifestyle, you've
got to change the car every two years.
People are worried now about their life
and I think in many ways this is
showing in their worry about things,
and then they're easily upset or easily
annoyed or they're on a cliff edge all the
time. Then going back to my lifestyle:
one of the real differences is you always
had a woman at home. Your mother was
at home, when you went home there
was somebody in the house, and there
was a pleasantness there. Dad came

Paddy McAteer on holiday, 1953.

Paddy McAteer on a Sunday Club outing in Co. Down, 1954.

Sheila Hughes in 1945.

home, he'd be tired, he'd done a day's work, and he sat and put his feet up. Mum dished up the dinner, and the kids enjoyed it; you know, there was a pleasantness, that is a difference now. Because the woman of the house, the mother now, is out working, working just as hard as her husband, and they're both coming back tired and weary, and the kids have been with their granny. Everything about today is stress and strain, and I think that shows.

*Paddy McAteer, born 1928*


## Less Respect

I was just relating to some friends of mine recently, that I was travelling in the train, and there was this old lady, older than I was. As I would have always done, as I'd been trained to do, I stepped up to let her sit down, and this young fella dived into the seat, and he knew she was standing there, and he must have wondered why I got up, but he got down in that seat. And I'm not blaming him as such, but it's just that difference that showed so clearly to me, that there's something terribly wrong. I was wondering: we always talk about the world going round in circles, and I'm wondering, will there be a reaction? Can we bring that sort of society back, because I do miss it. I think there was genteelness and friendliness. There's certainly still the friendliness but it's raw and it's rough and it's tough, and it's aggressive, and I just think things are changing, perhaps changing for the worse.

*Paddy McAteer, born 1928*


## Getting Older

As my friend said recently, 'You know, it's great, Peggy, isn't it?' You make up your face and then you put your glasses on, and you try not to overdo it, you realize that you're not seeing in the mirror exactly what's here. You try not to overdo it as far as make-up and things like that are concerned. I do go out to a lot of things, but I find I have to settle down and be on my own and try and recharge my batteries as it were. I keep trying to say to people in these various activities that I'm in, that it's going to be difficult for me. I've said that by the next September if I'm still around I'll be heading on for my eightieth birthday. So I mean I don't see myself being able to do all that's needing to be done, the organization of it.

*Peg Armstrong, born 1919*


## Growing Old

People sometimes tend to go by a figure, you know I am now seventy years of age, so I'm old. I don't think that at all. I don't feel one bit old; I get a shock mind you when I look in the mirror sometimes. But I feel very young inside and I can identify with young people, you know. I think young people these days are great, and I think they have an awful lot of demands upon them, much more so than I had, you know. I think of the temptations that young people have now, that I didn't have when I was young. If I had had to live through the temptations young people have now.... Everywhere they go there's alcohol, there's drugs now, you know I mean sexual permissiveness, all that. I was frightened when I was young, you know fear kept me from doing many things. Everything was black or it was white, it was right or wrong, you know; now, there's every shade of grey that you can imagine. And I think young people are wonderful, I really do, and I can identify with them very much indeed. But I think to keep a youthful outlook, if you like, is absolutely vital.

*Sheila Hughes, born 1928*

## National Insurance

When you look at my father, for instance, he went out and worked to bring my brother and me up, and getting no money at all in towards anything. If that was today he would have help of some sort, or, you know, my mother would be getting help of some sort. You'd be getting what you call the attendance allowance and all those things, but there was nothing like that in those days.

*Nessie McNamee, born 1921*

## Society Today

Obviously when you look back you remember the good times and you don't necessarily remember the bad times, so I only look back and see and remember the times that were great. I don't remember the boring times, the times of hard work, the times when you'd wish that you were back home again, I don't really remember those.

But I do think that there are huge changes that are taking place in community life, and changes that are taking place in family life. In family life there are enormous changes taking place, even within my own family: both my daughters are separated. There are the difficulties that that brings about, particularly when there are children involved as well, and I think that the concept of family life has changed, with the breakdown of family life and community life. Where one minute we're told this really has no effect, everybody's happy, but in actual fact now, evidence is starting to come out, that this is really not the case. I think that we need to have a radical look in the Millennium, a very radical look, to see what changes we need to bring into our lives.

*Clive Hughes, born 1939*

## Return to Family Life

Now the political parties, they are fooling around about the idea of family life now. I'm not too sure whether they're wanting to make these decisions on the basis of what's good for the country or whether they are wishing to make these decisions on what's good for their party. Both Hague and Blair are now talking about returning to the family values, and the return that they have. I'm not too sure that it may not be too late to replace the kind of family that I lived with, it may not be. It may be that I was not aware of the tensions within my own family, it may have been that. I can't see a different way of living outside a family. I cannot see how young

Maud Meneely with her father and daughter Pamela, in Tempo.

people with children don't need the support of families, the extended family round them. I think that we're going to have to revisit family life. Marriage doesn't make a family and I think that we have enormous changes that we're going to have to make and look at before we progress successfully into the next years.

*Clive Hughes, born 1939*

## Modern Life

In one sense the people are better cared for, you see, financially, but on the other side I would say that things are not going the best. I think they get along alright just the same but there is always that feeling in the background that you never know what's round the corner, what's going to stop all this.

Well of course smoking and pills, and drugs and drink, those are the fatal things for young people, and I think

Maureen Orchard-Smith (seated), with her colleagues at Belfast Women's Aid, 1999.

that it's ridiculous they should be allowed, and of course talking about sex – that's bad. They never should have allowed them to teach sex in school. But the drugs are the worst enemy of this generation, I would say, because what purpose do they fill?

I think not enough is done for children in the home. I think that the reason is that there are so many mothers working, they have no time for the children, they're not taught manners or anything like that. I can see my mother sitting at the table and she was talking: 'A knife is to cut with, a fork is to lift with, a spoon is to sup, you don't use those for anything else.' Now I see them eating off the knife – my mother would have murdered you if you had done that. It's not right.

There is no discipline at all and it's very difficult for the teacher, because the teacher only sees them so many hours in a day. The mother sees them the rest of the time, when she should be directing them, but she doesn't and because they're working themselves, children get to the pictures and they see things maybe they shouldn't see.

*Lena Purdy, born 1901*

Maureen Orchard-Smith at school.

Lina Graham in the mid-1950s.

## The Millennium

Obviously they don't understand the message of God, because some of the things that happen wouldn't have happened. But where there's life there's hope, and I think a lot of the people who are involved in terrorism, a good lot of them have changed and have regretted what they've done and I think it's coming that way. I think my hope for the new millennium would be that we would see real peace here.

It has a special meaning for me because it's two thousand years after the birth of Christ, and that's really what we ought to be celebrating. I don't suppose we all will be, but that's really what it's about, and I mean that has made such a change in the world that I think it is something worth celebrating.

The religious side gets very little attention really, and I'm wondering why the various churches haven't taken it up more. I have heard it mentioned very little in church, or in anybody writing or talking about it in the media at all. I mean they may talk about the millennium but not in the sense of what it really is celebrating.

*Maud Meneely, born 1929*

## Hope for the Future

You have to live in hope and I do have hope that there will be a big revival and we'll all be ready to meet it. I've always thought that because you've got to have faith, you've got to have hope, so you have, to hope in the future. Because what would you do if you had no faith or you had no hope?

I hope the true meaning of the Millennium is held, that it will not just be parties and things and that will be kept just like Christmas. The true meaning is of the Lord's birth. Like, I can enjoy Christmas but the Christ has went out of it for some people and I would like to see it brought in again. You know people are just trying to outdo one another. Although I love lights and I have a Christmas tree up every Christmas, I always remember the other side of it, you know, and I love getting presents. But some people just have that on their high priority, it's very materialized now.

It's just learnt me to be tolerant and understanding and just to help one another and just to listen to other people's views and that, and respect them. I never had any trouble anyway that way in religion.

*Nessie McNamee, born 1921*

## Role of Women

Women are taking a major part in everything, politics and, well, in general maybe. In a way I wonder sometimes if it's always a good thing, because I'm thinking of children, you know you look around and sometimes I wonder because there isn't the same discipline with regard to children. They're allowed to get away with so much, more than in my day. I mean my parents, they weren't strict; they were good because I respected them, I knew what I could do, and I knew what I can't. But when I see some of the children today, I think some of the parents they don't seem to bother, they don't seem to care the same, and I feel its such a pity, because I respected my parents. I wouldn't do some of the things that occur today, you know, because I know it would be wrong. Whereas today they just seem to please themselves so much. I think that sometimes maybe, they do miss the parents, because the mother is working. It's difficult, really, I know, because people want a good life, but at the same time I think the children are important. They should see more of both parents.

*Maureen Orchard-Smith, born 1924*

## Changes in my Lifetime

I was born in 1921 which makes me seventy-seven now, rather more than three-quarters of the century. My ambition is to survive another couple of years to see us into the next millennium. I have seen huge changes, many of them are to be deplored but probably more to be admired. I think that the province has progressed tremendously. Forget about the Troubles: it's a horrible period in our history. And people on both sides of the community behaved like madmen, but underneath it all the people of Northern Ireland are still the solid citizens that they always were. Their lot has improved, there's not the same amount of poverty; I know there's still hard times in places, but there's not the same poverty, there's certainly not the same fear of the future, that existed when I was a boy. It was because social security did not exist and if people hadn't looked after themselves there was the workhouse, or charity. That

disappeared of course in '48 with the founding of the welfare state. I know that there's still flaws in this scheme, but it's still basically something that other countries admire. Perhaps some people are too dependent on it, but basically we have progressed hugely. The people of the province have contributed a lot outside the province and within it... To see the development of computers, which are still a mystery to me, and yet my eight-year-old grandchild can operate it. The progress in welfare, society in general, the general quality of life, has improved.

*William Wright, born 1921*